GREEN POLITICS IN CHINA

Green Politics in China

Environmental Governance and
State–Society Relations

Joy Y. Zhang
and
Michael Barr

PlutoPress
www.plutobooks.com

First published 2013 by Pluto Press
345 Archway Road, London N6 5AA

www.plutobooks.com

Distributed in the United States of America exclusively by
Palgrave Macmillan, a division of St. Martin's Press LLC,
175 Fifth Avenue, New York, NY 10010

British Library Cataloguing in Publication Data
A catalogue record for this book is available from the British Library

ISBN 978 0 7453 3300 7 Hardback
ISBN 978 0 7453 3299 4 Paperback
ISBN 978 1 8496 4912 4 PDF eBook
ISBN 978 1 8496 4914 8 Kindle eBook
ISBN 978 1 8496 4913 1 EPUB eBook

Library of Congress Cataloging in Publication Data applied for

This book is printed on paper suitable for recycling and made from fully managed and
sustained forest sources. Logging, pulping and manufacturing processes are expected to
conform to the environmental standards of the country of origin.

10 9 8 7 6 5 4 3 2 1

Typeset by Curran Publishing Services, Norwich
Simultaneously printed digitally by CPI Antony Rowe, Chippenham, UK and
Edwards Bros in the United States of America

CONTENTS

ABBREVIATIONS

AFSC	American Friends Service Committee
CAI-Asia	Clean Air Initiative for Asian Cities
CDM	Clean Development Mechanism
COP17	17th Conference of the Parties on Climate Change
ENGO	environmental non-governmental organisation
EPB	environmental protection bureau
FYP	Five-Year Plan
GDP	gross domestic product
GHG	greenhouse gas
GONGO	government-organised NGOs
INGO	international NGO
IPE	Institute of Public and Environmental Affairs
MEP	Ministry of Environmental Protection,
NDRC	National Development and Reform Commission
NEC	National Energy Commission
NGO	non-governmental organisation
NNR	national natural reserve
NPC	National People's Congress
PE	The Pacific Environment
PM	particulate matter
UNFCCC	United Nations Framework Convention on Climate Change
WHO	World Health Organization

ACKNOWLEDGEMENTS

The research for this book was funded by la Fondation Maison des Sciences de l'Homme (FMSH). It forms part of the Cosmopolitan Risk Communities research programme, based at le Collège d'Etudes Mondiales, Paris. We are deeply grateful to Professor Michel Wieviorka for his support. Our warm thanks also go to Dr Angela Procoli for her Parisian hospitality and to David Castle at Pluto Press, for his patience and encouragement.

We also wish to thank our interviewees, without whom this book would not have been possible. We are especially indebted to FYF, WXZ and SN for their help in making some of the interviews possible. And last but not least, we also thank AC and TDE for making the endless travel a bit easier.

Joy Y. Zhang
Michael Barr

INTRODUCTION

'Hollywood got it all wrong,' said Chen Qi, a hydraulic engineer from Shenzhen. He was referring to the movie 2012, in which humans face extinction because of a series of natural disasters. In Chen's view, the film's biggest mistake was to build Noah's Ark on the Tibetan plateau. 'The movie assumed Tibet as the last safe place on Earth, but in the face of climate change, the "roof of the world" will actually be among the first to be affected!' Chen had a stack of empirical data to back up his argument. These data were collected not through his formal job as engineer but as a volunteer for Green River, a Sichuan-based environmental non-governmental organisation (ENGO). The data set consisted of records from local metrology offices and independent water sampling tests from 2003 in the Tuotuo river area on the Tibetan Plateau. It is a region of vital importance for environmental security since the plateau serves as the source of the Yangtze River, whose waters help enable China to account for 35 per cent of the world's rice production.

In fact, Chen and his fellow Green River volunteers also brought these data to the 17th Conference of the Parties on Climate Change (COP17) held in Durban. An observer organisation for the United Nations Framework Convention on Climate Change (UNFCCC) since 2009, Green River is known for its voluminous data collection and analysis. During COP17, Green River shared new findings on the impact of climate change, especially the degrading water quality at the source of the Yangtze (Green River, 2012). But Chen and his friends did not present their work in technical statistics or intricate graphs. They framed the data within the narrative of the 'silent sheep' – meaning the sheep that were unable to speak for their physical pain caused by polluted water and malnourishment. Green River's study found that while there had been little variation in annual precipitation rates in this area, the form of precipitation had notably shifted from snow to rain, with an increased occurrence of torrential rain. Chen's hypothesis was that the change in weather patterns might have washed a higher amount of Tibet's mineral-rich surface soil into the nearby rivers. The high mineral content of the water may have caused the sheep to be ill as the local farmers, affected by severe stomach ailments, had long opted for an alternative water source for their own consumption. When we interviewed Chen in early 2012, he was hoping further research would verify his tentative explanation. As a hydraulic engineer, he was meticulous in giving valid and reliable scientific conclusions. However, he was also keen to not lose time in publicising his initial hypothesis and data on degrading water quality in the source region of the Yangtze River. 'It is not simply about a gradual change of water quality at a sparsely populated area,' explained Chen, 'but it is pollution of the source of a river that runs through China, serving as the key water supply to approximately one third of China's population!' For Chen, there were two types of environment challenges:

> Most people are familiar with the rhetoric of catastrophic 'what if' scenarios in well-known cities: Shanghai immersed in water or Beijing buried in sand storms etc. The incalculable economic loss alone would be a reason for action. But I feel sometimes we are blinded from environmental challenges that are not in the spotlight but may have more profound and much wider implications for Chinese society.

Chen and his ENGO friends were concerned about obvious 'headline concerns', but they were more worried about those less visible and perhaps more significant environmental impacts that plague Chinese people on a daily basis – such as the potential harms which have quietly slipped into China's soil from changing patterns of precipitation.

We use Chen's experience as an introduction because this book holds a similar ambition to his environmental work. We hope to shed light on significant but less talked-about issues in Chinese environmental politics. For most people living in China, environmental consequences are not 'what if' mind exercises, but are everyday confrontations in the food they eat, the water they bathe in, the air they breathe, and the lifestyle they choose. Thus, apart from Chinese government policies and pledges, this book aims to make visible how the struggle for environmental rights has entered the life of ordinary Chinese citizens. As a consequence of this, we show how green politics in China has led to a pluralisation of political participation, and in some cases, has revolutionised China's civil sphere. To be sure, none of the efforts from civil society are (yet) comparable to the leverage the government has in directing environmental actions. However, it is increasingly clear that while Chinese politicians hold unrivalled power, their capacity to control and steer the greening of China is increasingly being challenged and open to negotiation. In other words, this book aims to bring to the foreground what has largely been in the background.

Stepping into Muddy Water

There are three themes of primary interest to this book. They are also, to varying degrees, themes that are exhibited in our example of Chen Qi. First, we are concerned with the geography of 'imagined communities' in China (Anderson, 1983). We argue that how connections between actors are conceived and perceived underpins issues of rights and responsibilities in environmental conflicts. The mapping, or the 'geography', of social relatedness provides essential insights to the rationales of green agendas. While NIMBYism ('not in my backyard'), or localised opposition to a particular environmental concern, is a common incentive for public participation, the conceptual premises of what constitutes a 'backyard' and its recognised stakeholders may take on a fluid and open-ended nature (Johnson, 2010; Feng, 2010). For example, it may seem puzzling why Chen, a regular consultant for urban planning projects in the southeastern city Shenzhen, became a volunteer of a mid-west ENGO, committing two months every year to understanding the underdeveloped far west of China, 3,800 kilometres away. But it made sense to Chen as he considered the Yangtze source region as the 'backyard' to the well-being of people on the east coast. In addition, the tension surrounding the distribution of environmental responsibilities between the Yangtze delta and the upstream Tibetan plateau can be seen as a larger-scale replica of the situation within the Pearl River delta, where Chen's home in Shenzhen is situated.

To be sure, global communication and the ease of international travel have made the world small. But it is only the interrelatedness between one's fate and that of the domestic and global Other that shrinks political distance and reconfigures the contours of domination. Thus while this book is about 'China', it does not presuppose a national/international or China versus the world binary. Rather, we seek to explore the social imagination of communities present in Chinese green initiatives.

The second theme addresses the entangled social webs which enable environment action in China. Doing research on Chinese grassroots politics is almost like stepping into muddy water. Even basic questions, such as how many non-government organisations (NGOs) exist in China, or whether or not the country even has 'true' NGOs, lack clear answers and are enthusiastically debated (Frolic, 1997; Knup, 1997; Ma, 2002, 2005; Schwartz, 2004; Tang and Zhan, 2008). However this book argues that the search for 'purity' may be misleading, as reality is always messy. There is rarely a singular or linear relationship amongst the movers and the shakers of social development. Thus, this book recognises the complexity of social influence and acknowledges that social actors often have multiple identities.

For example, in Chen's case, apart from being a hydraulic engineer and a green activist, he is also a local committee member of the Jiusan Society, one of the eight legally recognised political parties in China. The goal of Chen's work is not simply to contribute his professional knowledge to ENGOs or to take his findings to COP17 in Durban. His efforts also underlie his annual policy proposals to the Shenzhen government as a Jiusan committee member. Chen told us that on at least one occasion his environmental proposals have prompted an official response from the mayor of Shenzhen. But in addition to this, he was also keen on disseminating NGO findings to his colleagues in engineering, who were a receptive audience. Thus, Chen is at the nexus of at least three important communities to green politics: NGOs, scientific professionals and politicians. While this may not be unique, the implications of these overlapping roles are not often explored.

Third, this book identifies a series of innovative mobilisation strategies employed by Chinese stakeholders, especially those at the grassroots. At one level, this means better communicative skills and narrative building, such as how Chen packaged his concerns in a story of 'silent sheep' rather than displaying endless scientific figures. But more importantly, as is demonstrated in later chapters, Chinese environmentalists are keen to develop new ways to engage with diverse audiences, mobilise social resources, and compete for political influence. In this sense, green civil society in China is helping to make the rules, rather than merely follow them (Mertha, 2010).

Shades of Green: Balancing Development and Social Stability

China's unprecedented economic growth comes with a heavy environmental cost. According to 2012 government statistics, around 40 per cent of China's fresh water resources still pose a health risk to the public (MEP, 2012). A 2007 report by the World Bank and China's State Environmental Protection Administration (later known as the Ministry of Environmental Protection, MEP) estimated that the damages associated with air pollution alone amounted to 3.8 per cent of China's gross domestic product (GDP) (World Bank and SEPA, 2007). And as is well known, air travels. Many have expressed concerns about the potential harms of 'living downwind of China' (Zhang et al., 2010: 1111–13). Such expressions do little for China's international image. The list could go on. The outflow of pollution from industrial to rural regions, for example, has threatened China's food security and put at risk its exports to the West. Indeed, China's impact on the global environment is well established. Over the past decade, China's carbon dioxide emissions have increased by 150 per cent (Olivier, Janssens-Maenhout and Peters, 2012: 11). While it has relatively low per capita emissions in absolute terms, China is the world's biggest energy consumer and the world largest emitter of greenhouse gases, accounting for 29 per cent of total global carbon emissions (Swartz and Oster, 2010; Olivier et al., 2012: 6).

In both media and academic discussions, optimism and scepticism, acclaim and blame seem to coexist regarding China's potential in global environmental mitigation. China is portrayed simultaneously as a reckless polluter and as an emerging leader. On the one hand, there exist many optimists who draw attention to China's commitment to environmental technology. In the eyes of this group (including many innovators and investors), China 'gets it' in a way that many Western nations still do not. That is, China is aggressively tying its future energy security to ambitious environmental projects. Already a world leader in wind turbine and solar panel production (Bradsher, 2010), China is seen as leading 'by action, as opposed to seeking binding commitments at international conferences' (China Green Initiative, 2011:12, 46). A second, more pessimistic, school of thought reminds us that China is still effectively an authoritarian one-party state. Many in this camp doubt the sustainability and fairness of government-supported projects, as well as the actual social impact of these showcase initiatives. For example, some suspect that China is not committed to 'green tech' per se, but that its so-called climate initiatives are primarily economically driven. Development will always trump environmental protection, the sceptics argue (Lo, 2010).

To make sense of the mixed, sometimes contradictory, views on China's role in global environment politics, it is necessary to understand the internal transformations that the green movement has brought within China, and how the notion of 'going green' is employed by Chinese stakeholders in pushing the boundaries of political participation. We begin by exploring the broader context to China's green movement, which can be described as a juggling act between development and social stability.

'Sustainable Development' with Chinese Characteristics

'*Tian-ren heyi*', the unity of human and nature, is a key concept in Chinese traditional philosophy. It was also an idea frequently mentioned by the various Chinese stakeholders we talked to. A common refrain went like this: 'Yes, it's true that modern industrialisation is anthropocentric and Nature is alienated as a means to serve human purpose. But we should also remember that a compassionate and respectful attitude towards nature is an idea that has been embedded in Chinese traditional thinking since 700 BC.' The point in bringing up this ancient wisdom was to attest that although China's environment was in a dire situation, there was reason for optimism. The 'main direction' (*da fangxiang*) in Chinese consciousness was to transcend a narrow focus on economic gains in favour of a harmony between humans and nature.

However, looking at China's development trajectory, this commonly expressed view sounds more nostalgic than convincing. The environment is not a recent topic in China. A well-known policy, often cited within China, is the move in the 1970s to recycle the 'three industrial wastes' (*sanfei*: that is, waste water, waste gas and waste residue), with the aim of improving economic efficiency (L.H. Zhang, 2011). Even prior to this, in the 1950s, at the very beginning of the founding of the People's Republic, the environment was already an important issue for Chinese policy makers. Yet policies often contradicted one another. For example, Mao Zedong launched a large-scale, government-directed afforestation project, which has been renewed by every generation of Chinese leaders to the present day (Yang, 2011). Yet one consequence of the Great Leap Forward (1958–62) was widespread deforestation, as trees were cut to help fuel the 'backyard furnaces' that Mao hoped would propel China ahead of the West in industrial production. In Mao's view, it was desirable to bend the physical world to human will. Many of his policies reflect this urge. The 'Four Pests Campaign' for example aimed to eliminate rats, flies, mosquitoes and sparrows, but had the effect of upsetting the ecological balance and enabled the proliferation of crop-eating insects (Shapiro, 2001).

China's green initiatives, whatever their effects, cannot be taken at face value. The master plan of economic development has been clear from the beginning. Industrial waste management was initially targeted for better economic efficiency and expansion of resources (L.H. Zhang, 2011). The aim of China's environment governance was thus 'to slow down environmental deterioration but, not to stop it' (Tang and Zhan, 2008: 430). Meanwhile, afforestation was seen not as a primarily ecological concern, but rather as an economic one (Jiang, 2007; L.P. Wang, 2007; Feng, 2008). The masses were encouraged to turn 'wild land' into rubber plantations or plant fast-growing timber. From many of China's highways, you can see these trees standing in uniformity like People's Liberation Army soldiers. This is because, for cultural and aesthetic reasons, these forests are nearly always single-species. Pinaceae trees in particular are the preferred choice in many parts of China because they remain green all year round and have cultural implications of long life and good luck. Yet monocultured woodlands lack diversity and are ecologically more vulnerable to pathogens and insects. So although China now has the world's largest forest planted by humans, covering 53 million hectares, such a triumph has been achieved through clearing wild (that is more diverse) forests in favour of aesthetically pleasing monospecies (Liu, 2009). In other words, afforestation has led to de facto deforestation.

This perverse pragmatism continues today. The Chinese government is criticised for seeing climate change policy 'not as a cross-sectoral environmental issue, but largely an economic one' (Yang, 2009: 1013). For example, China is currently the world's leading recipient of the United Nations Clean Development Mechanism (CDM) programme (Schroeder, 2009). The CDM is an international market mechanism which allows emission-reduction projects in developing countries to earn emission reduction credits, which can be traded and used by industrialised countries to a meet their emission reduction targets under the Kyoto Protocol. Countries that host CDM projects benefit from technology transfer and from projects which help achieve sustainable development. When CDM was first launched, China 'showed little enthusiasm' and had limited participation. This changed as it became clear that in addition to the environmental benefits, hosting CDM projects could also have financial rewards (Shin, 2010; Shen, 2011).

As we discuss in Chapter 5, China's five-year plans are another good example of the complicated nexus between development and environmental protection. The 11th Five-Year Plan (2006–10) was commonly described as a 'turning point' in which restructuring China's energy consumption and developing renewable energy were highlighted (Fan, 2006). But the plan also seemed to reconfirm an economic-focus behind China's green initiatives. One policy analyst at the Climate Policy Initiative at Tsinghua University recounted that China's decisiveness in revolutionising its energy structure was not so much a result of 'international pressure on climate change', but rather 'self-initiated'. In 2002, for example, China's energy intensity – units of energy spent per unit of GDP – started to rise dramatically. This coincided with an increasingly uncertain geopolitical context after September 11, 2001. In 2011, China imported roughly 45 per cent of its crude oil supply, most of it sourced from the Middle East, and then transported through the Indian Ocean (IEA, 2012). Thus, as we discuss later, the Chinese government has been incentivised to reform the means of economic development, especially how it (literally) fuels its continued rise.

To be sure, for China, a country in which 29.8 per cent of the population still needs to be lifted above the $2.00 a day poverty line (World Bank, 2009a), development is essential. But the extent of its ecological degradation is now causing many to question the means by which China develops. Increasingly within China, the desire for economic growth and the basic demand for a healthy environment are not seen as mutually exclusive goals. However, these issues pose a concern for the government, which bases its legitimacy on sustained economic growth.

'Sustainable development' seems to be an obvious solution to the Chinese dilemma. But in practice, 'sustainability' is subject to different interpretations. This is not unique to China, but the need for social and political sustainability is perhaps more acute in China. It is worth remembering that despite 30 years of 11 per cent economic growth, China still suffers from a huge development gap, a situation famously described by economist Hu Angang as 'one China, four worlds' (Hu, 2002). Politically, it is also a country that has much less centralised power than is commonly assumed. In fact, China 'is more like Europe ... a thin political union composed of semiautonomous cities – some with as many inhabitants as a European country' (Bell, 2012).

The difference between a 'universal' definition of sustainability and a Chinese one may provide some insights on China's perspective. Globally speaking, the idea of 'sustainable development' was coined in the 1987 publication *Our Common Future*, also known as the Brundtland Report, from the United Nations World Commission on

Environment and Development (WCED, 1987). This notion directs the world to a seek mode of development that 'meets the needs of the present without compromising the ability of future generations to meet their own needs'. Here, sustainability is first and foremost viewed as a temporal attribute to social advancement, with assuring cross-generational equality as the core aim. In Chinese discussions, this concept is given a spatial dimension as well. That is, in addition to the rights of future generations, development is only considered sustainable if 'it meets the needs of a region or a nation without endangering the ability of people in other regions and nations to meet their own needs' (Wang, 2002: 327).

China's definition of sustainable development is in line with its emphasis on 'common but differentiated responsibilities', the phrase used to signify the view that while every nation has climate-related obligations, some countries have more responsibilities than others given their level of development and their role in creating global warming to begin with. The added weight given to the need for 'other' regions to develop reflects not only a concern for the less well-off, but also an apprehension in attending to existing social gaps, both domestic and global. As was rightly pointed out by Peter Ho (2006), going green and embarking on sustainability may not necessarily convey the same target in the Chinese context. In other words, for China, sustainability in economic development is not limited to being ecologically sustainable, but also reflects a search for politically and socially sustainable programmes. Viewed in this way, it may not be surprising to see that 'sustainable' development is sometimes seen as equal to 'do-able' development.

Another example is the findings of the Green Long March (*Lvse Changzheng*), a national youth programme which aims to promote sustainable development (www.future.org). Xue Yan, a 22-year-old university graduate, was given the task of surveying 100 enterprises the northwestern city of Lanzhou, one of China's most polluted urban areas. According to Xue, nine out of ten factories rejected her visit, fearing she was an undercover inspector, or worse, a journalist. But there were some local businesses that opened their doors to her. To Xue's initial surprise, quite a large number of these welcoming factories were far from being environment-friendly. Xue was shown around the factories and witnessed outdated equipment which created unnecessary pollution. She found that most of the factory managers knew that they were causing serious environmental problems. In fact, they were 'quite frank about it' and often had a clear idea of what equipment needed to be replaced and what new technologies ought to be introduced. What was more interesting was the conclusion Xue drew from this study: 'the factory managers were not really the ones to blame'. According to this young volunteer, there was a more serious problem underlying local pollution:

> Of course business should take on their social responsibilities, but they are also pressured to generate revenue and keep up the local employment rate. There are those who welcome going green, but are trapped with no financial or social resources. There are bigger administrative and social issues that need to be dealt with to enable local businesses to afford a choice.

In fact, these 'guilt-free' polluters are not uncommon in China. Their stories can be found in newspapers and magazines, and were a key theme in one of China's first novels with an environmental theme, *Director of the Environment Bureau* (Li, 2009). Many of these businesses, inefficient as they are, still serve as essential bloodlines for local economies. But as we show in Chapter 3, the pressure for 'getting rich' is not unique to small chemical factories or local refineries in the underdeveloped western China. Similar pressures exist in the seemingly high-end factories along the east coast.

To summarise, the concern for economic growth and short-term gains still casts a shadow on China's green initiatives at the national, local and personal levels. But as Xue's example demonstrates, it also necessitates a reflection on the relations between society, industry and the state, as well as a reconsideration of the distribution of power and responsibility, the right to have a say and the right to be heard.

Revolution from Within: Changing State–Society Relations

In comparison to the central government, citizen-organised ENGOs in China are a recent phenomenon. They started mainly as nature conservation organisations and watchdogs for local air and water pollution (Schroeder, 2008). The first organisation of this kind was Friends of Nature, founded in 1994. It served as the 'mother organisation' in the sense that a number of its early members later set up ENGOs of their own. By the end of 1990s, there was a palpable increase in international NGOs (INGOs) in China, which exerted an important influence on the rise of civil society. In many cases, homegrown NGOs founded during this period were led by individuals who either studied in the West or had 'simply worked in an INGO before setting up their own organisations' (Chen, 2010: 508). As we might expect, ENGOs need to adapt to the political particularities of China. This can be seen from the official interpretation of the term 'NGO'. As one study pointed out, 'the Chinese official definition of NGOs does not mention self-governance, a key criteria of Western nongovernmental organisations' (Ma, 2005). But increasingly the Chinese government has recognised the importance of civil organisations in filling the gaps in government services and mitigating social conflicts. Thus, NGOs in China have a strange form, often as government-organised NGOs (GONGOs). As we discuss in Chapter 4, given the high standards for NGO registration, it is common for many organisations to remain unregistered, or as they are sometimes, and misleadingly, described, 'underground'. Yang Hongming, an environmental sociologist in Beijing summarised the situation as follows:

There are many grassroots ENGOs in China, but few have a legitimate status. Many are in the form of business, and register with the local Administration for Industry and Commerce, instead of the Bureau of Civil Affairs. In theory, all domestic ENGOs are members of the umbrella organisation, the China Environment Protection Foundation. It officially has a few thousand ENGOs, but in fact there may be tens of thousands of unregistered grassroots organizations.

The central government has adopted differentiated strategies towards social organizations in relation to their perceived political antagonism. Beijing takes a very different approach to Falun Gong, for example, than it does to most commercially associated NGOs (Kang and Han, 2008). It maintains its influence over non-state actors through corporatism – that is, a system whereby it establishes itself as the arbitrator of legitimacy by limiting and licensing the number of players with which it must negotiate its policies, essentially co-opting their leadership into policing their own members (Hsu and Hasmath, 2012). To survive, ENGOs must avoid the appearance of threatening the structural status quo. However, the heavy interface between the two groups allows NGOs to play a more significant role in the political process than might otherwise be the case. Many corporatist analyses assume that governments in authoritarian states are able to act uniformly to ensure control over civil society. As we shall see, this is not necessarily true. Given this context, there are two common perceptions of China's state–society relations regarding environment protection. One stresses the dominant role of the Chinese central government, which is still in control of substantial financial and social resources. The other highlights that ENGOs are 'hopeful' advocates, trapped in an authoritarian state.

Although both claims have some truth to them, measuring the power of Chinese ENGOs against the government may be missing the point. For the value of an emerging civil society in China is not to have a new form of authority to replace the existing one. Rather, NGOs serve to help pluralise the political process. To be sure, there are examples when civil efforts have had a clear impact on environmental governance. In 2004, the Nujiang hydropower station was put on hold because of Wang Yongchen's campaign (Lu, 2007). More recently, protests in Ningbo helped stop plans to expand a petrochemical complex (Waldmeir, Hook and Anderlini, 2012). However, the impact of civil society cannot be measured in immediate policy outcomes. Instead, it must be seen in the wider social-political behaviour organisations cultivate.

It is true that the civic functions of Chinese green NGOs are often dismissed, for they are seen as being limited to low-impact events such as environmental public education campaigns, hosting online chatrooms, or handing out brochures (Yang, 2009; Shin, 2010). However, it is also true that for China, a country in which government-controlled media was once the only real source of information, grassroots attempts to spread environmental knowledge are 'a big deal'. They could be regarded within China as the first large-scale public engagement with science promoted from the bottom up. NGOs publish not only energy-saving handbooks and translated Western scientific leaflets, but also live online reports on food contamination, work plant pollution, new building construction and waste site dumps. The reports, which are compiled from dispersed sources and sometimes deeply buried government papers, equip local citizens with a first line of defence towards environmental hazards. As many of the case studies in this book suggest, the trend towards public disclosure of environment information and the general defence of the 'right to know', are both empowering and daring.

Although Chinese activists clearly acknowledge the government as the dominant actor, this is not necessarily a form of political submission. In line with other research, most activists we interviewed suggested that their stance is best understood as a form of pragmatic realism, for sometimes 'it is necessary to work from *within* the nexus of power in order to make a difference'(Ho, 2001: 917–18, original emphasis). It is useful to bear in mind that for those living in China, problems such as industrial pollution, food security and ecological degradation are often immediate worries that affect their daily well-being. Courting government approval is undeniably a more effective way to solve problems than outright confrontation with the state.

For example, the booming housing market in China has pressured local officials into a slippery slope of compromises to ease environmental standards. In the last few years, the official safety distance of a waste incineration plant to residential buildings has shortened from 200 metres to 70 metres (Feng, 2008). In 2009, a young woman in Beijing sued both the disposal company and the local trash office for air pollution. Her aim was to send a strong message to the authorities rather than seek personal compensation, for which she only asked for 300RMB (£30). The first of its kind, this case attracted much attention among urban property owners. But such activism is not only found among middle-class city dwellers; it can also be found in groups traditionally considered disadvantaged. One such example is Chen Faqing, a farmer who is known for exploiting existing legal channels in subjecting irresponsible authorities and factory plants to justice, and for promoting China's public interest litigation reform.[1]

'Environment protection is a war that can never be won. We fight, not so much because we are in search of victory, but in defiance of despair' (Tang, quoted in Feng, 2011: 320–1). This is a quote from Tang Xiyang, who founded the National College Student Green Camps, known as the 'West Point' Academy of Chinese environment protection. To comprehend China's green movement, it is perhaps as important to understand its practical goals as much as the 'despair' it fights against and the hope it aims to retain.

A New 'United Front'

Perhaps the green movement can be characterised as a form of warfare – not in the sense of hostility or conquering, but in the sense that it is a sustained campaign against an undesirable situation. It does not necessarily call for an 'us-against-them' antagonism. Rather it requires the formation of solidarities in a common struggle to defend the shared pursuit of a good life, a point we demonstrate in Chapters 2 and 3. One example is from an ENGO founder in

---

1 See Chen Faqing's website: <www.nmcfq.com>.

Beijing, Tang Peng. Tang has worked on environment protection for more than a decade. In describing China's green future to us, he used the term 'united front', which refers to when the Communists and Kuomintang set aside their civil war in order to wage battle together, first against warlordism and then against the Japanese. Tang elaborated what he meant:

> There are social resources and social energies that are in deep sleep in China. Environmental protection here must have the ability to somehow transform these social resources, those people around you, into a sustainable force. If one only talks and acts within one's own circle, then you are stuck with your own imagination and your own limits. One needs to learn to employ a combination of methods to interact with what I termed the 'social biological system' [as opposed to the 'natural biological system']. Campaigning for policy changes is only one possible action to take. There are also other changes that can and should be made. The key test of an NGO's capacity is to what extent it can assimilate external social resources. That is, once a potential is in your hands, do you have the ability to recognise, incorporate and develop it into a force to solve actual problems?

As Tang pointed out, the implications for the green movement in China are not limited to 'green' itself, but also extend to the reinvigoration of a 'social biological system' that has partly been in 'deep sleep'. As with many countries, environmental protection in China has stimulated wider social contributions. At least in the eyes of Tang, the aim of Chinese ENGOs should not be to establish a social sphere, in which environment-friendly people 'act within their own circle'. Rather, actual problem solving relies on the ability of connecting different social spheres into a united front.

This spirit of collaboration and alliance-forming in promoting the greening of China was also shared by other social actors. A number of academics we interviewed have established various working relations with ENGOs, from one-off consultations, to long-term volunteering, to co-organising events and data sharing. One researcher, whose work focused on automobile emissions standards, contributed to several air quality initiatives organised by ENGOs. He described relations with civil society as follows:

> We are in a relation based on mutual benefits. We as academics

have our goals, such as increasing research impact and attracting funding. They [the ENGOs] have their respective aims too. I'm not too concerned about their particular goal. All it matters is that in this phase, we can work for the environmental cause together.

The role of academics is especially important in China's green movement. This is not only because many leading environmentalists have the background of 'well-educated urban professionals' (Yang, 2009:124), but also because academics serve as key communicators and mediators between state and society. For example, one of the most comprehensive climate governance reviews in China is the *Blue Book of Low Carbon Development*, an annual publication compiled and published by the Climate Policy Initiative at Tsinghua University. What makes the *Blue Book* special is that even though it is an annual review of everything in the low-carbon field, pooling data from all available sources, it is written in accessible language for a well-informed public audience. It is not a book in service of the government, to keep officials updated with what is happening in the field. Rather, the *Blue Book* can be seen as a push for the sharing of data across isolated research centres, and for publicising what the government has done. One of the key contributors of the book told us that its direct policy impact was limited, but it nonetheless exerted important regulatory influence. The reason was that Chinese policy making is not about making arguments in order to secure votes, but about creating consensus among the decision makers. Thus the *Blue Book*'s value lies in bringing together data that are of mutual interest to both state and society.

The relations between government and civil groups are more entangled than simple repression or non-interference. As demonstrated in Chapter 4, the grassroots have a more practical view of the role of the state than commonly assumed. Government institutions at different levels have made a slow start in appreciating civil efforts. A few of our interviewees have been invited by various government institutions, as representatives, consultants or speakers in public events. One reason is that a non-governmental voice often adds credibility to the same argument being made by government officials.

This united front implies a key in understanding China's green politics: conflictual relations may not necessarily be antagonistic. Actors can still stage confrontational challenges without necessarily being antithetical to the government. Similarly, government could still be authoritarian while retreating in certain aspects of social control. This book hopes to challenge a static view of state–society relations in China. It demonstrates that governmental and non-governmental organisations, and organisations in the grey area between the two, each maintain their independence while at the same time often working together to transform China from within.

This new 'united front' may be better described as a 'united but not binding' front. That is, while there is a shared understanding that transboundary collaboration is needed in establishing new sociopolitical responses to the environment, such bonds between actors (that is, individual activists, NGOs, academics, media, enterprises, government institutions) are fluid as they are constantly steered and renewed by various self-interests.

Green Politics in China

The fieldwork for *Green Politics in China* took place between late 2011 and the middle of 2012. During this time we conducted 32 interviews from 14 different organisations across China. These included research institutes, student associations, registered civic NGOs, and underground NGOs. Most interviews were conducted in person, however a few were carried out via Skype or over the telephone. We are grateful that respondents were generous with their time, patient with our questions, and eager to discuss their work with us. To ensure the confidentiality of our interviewees, we have used pseudonyms throughout. The only exception to this are cases where the link between the individual and their organisation is already well established in the public domain.

As suggested above, *Green Politics in China* addresses the relationship between civil society and the party/state, explaining the manifold ways in which ENGOs are attempting to influence environmental policy. We do not seek to provide a fully comprehensive report on the current status of China's environment. There are no doubt important themes that we only touch upon in passing. Our aim, as hinted above, is to put the reader in the shoes of people living in China, especially those who have dedicated portions of their lives to protecting China's environment. This book joins a growing body of literature on Chinese environmental state–society relations. Many of our findings support this work, as we make clear throughout.

Chapter 1 addresses the question of blame. China seems increasingly unhappy: from climate sceptics, to government negotiators, to people affected by natural and human-made disasters, there is a growing chorus of voices demanding to know who is responsible for environmental risk and who is going to take the lead in doing something about it.

Chapter 2 challenges the view that public education is a weak form of green activism. We illustrate the novel ways in which ENGOs employ visual imagery to raise environmental consciousness. Using examples from natural photography, bird watching and a campaign to save Kekexili (Hoh Xil) in Tibet from commercial exploitation, we show how alternative forms of mobilisation and public engagement are changing the ways in which the environment is viewed within China.

We discuss the political dispute over PM2.5 air quality measures in Beijing and efforts to stop illegal dumping by the Chinese suppliers to Apple Inc. in Chapter 3. These examples show the heterogeneous ways in which ENGOs frame their campaigns and seek support. Whereas the first case relied on a bottom-up discourse of national pride to improve China's air quality, in the example of IT giant Apple, Chinese activists sought transnational collaboration with US-based NGOs. We conclude that grassroots environmental actors can be a greater force for change than they are often given credit for.

In Chapter 4 we examine how ENGOs situate themselves within China's political context. What are the potential benefits of officially registering with the government? What are the risks of not registering? How do environmental groups maintain staff levels when pay and social status are both low? We examine the multi-layered relationship between ENGOs and the government, and find that civil society actors can be characterised as both rebels and conformists.

Once we have explored ENGOs in some detail, Chapter 5 changes gears and looks at the role of the central government. China's fragmented system often inhibits the implementation of green initiatives yet its authoritarian approach has its advantages in the eyes of some. We examine what Beijing is doing to improve China's environment by analysing the 12th Five-Year Plan, circular economies, eco-cities, and the Party's call to build an ecological civilization. Finally, we conclude with an analysis of some of the changes key actors – the government, civil society and individuals – have had to embrace and will need to embrace if a green society is to be realised within China.

1 WHO IS TO BLAME?

Chinese Climate Sceptics: Recounting Responsibility?

Environment politics and climate change have generated huge volumes of academic and public debate. However, a YouTube video cleverly captures the gist of the issues in a mere 83-second cartoon. The cartoon shows that the core of 'climate negotiations' in the past two decades is a negotiation of responsibilities. Flags of various countries pass around a pair of scissors – used to symbolize cutting emissions – like a hot potato. While most countries agreed in principle that levels of carbon dioxide must be lowered, the question is who should mitigate and how? Developing countries blame the developed for their historical emissions: 'You caused it. You fix it,' chimes the cartoon. The North pressures the South with responsible development: 'Either all cut or I won't', says a sceptical-looking figure wrapped in an American flag, a large cigar burning from each corner of its mouth. The video ends with the countries striking a deal: the rich will pay the poor to cut their emissions so they don't have to.[1]

The video expresses a common sentiment within China, where, unbeknown to many in the West, a unique form of 'climate sceptics' has appeared. These sceptics do not challenge the validity of climate science per se. Instead they doubt the necessity and effectiveness of carbon reduction schemes. In their eyes, calls for low-carbon societies merely reflect the political and technical hegemony of the West. In 2010 alone, three books bearing provocative titles were published in China: *Low-Carbon Plot: China's vital war with the US and Europe* (Gou, 2010), *In the Name of CO_2: Global rivalry behind the low-carbon deceptions* (Liu, 2010), and *The Carbon Empire: Carbon capitalism and our bible* (Bai, 2010). All these titles aimed to inform the general public of a 'carbon colonialism' which

---

1 <See www.youtube.com/watch?v=B11kASPfYxY>.

endangered social and economic progress in less-advantaged areas of China.

It may not be difficult to understand why going green is framed by these sceptics as a form of global economic rivalry. It is common knowledge, for example, that the global production chain has enabled a 'dislocation of environment degradation' in which developed countries ship emission-heavy manufacturing jobs to developing countries (Rathzel and Uzzell, 2009). For example, China's Pearl River delta economic zone alone produces more than 60 per cent of the world's toys, and has been the global manufacturing base for footwear, lighting fixtures, furniture and automobile parts (HKTDC, 2011). In other words, many of this region's emissions are created for the benefit of consumers in developed countries. In this way, China is not only the world's factory in that it makes things; it is also the world's factory in the sense that it makes the pollution which allows the West to enjoy these things.

But these low-carbon conspiracy theorists are not only nationalistic or anti-West. Some of the scepticism of the carbon discourse also incorporates an uneasy scrutiny upon the Chinese domestic situation. For example, in its opening chapter, *The Low-Carbon Plot* questioned Beijing's commitment to the development of solar panels:

> Is solar power really clean? Investigations show that the base silicon that solar panels rely on is extracted via a energy intensive, heavily polluting industry. And where is this industry based? China .... China has already become the world's biggest photo-voltaic industrial market. The most important ingredient in solar power is polycrystalline silicon. The efficiency of manufacturing the panels is rather low, and a lot of pollution is generated as a by-product. When local industries started producing polycrystalline silicon, they were mostly reliant on outdated technology. Apart from high energy consumption, for every ton of pure polycrystalline silicon created, there were also more than 8 tons of silicon tetrachloride as by-product, as well as silicochloroform, chlorine gas and other waste water and waste gas .... The prosperity of China's solar power industry comes with the price of the environment of those rather weak distant regions. In order to attract investment and to collect tax revenue, many environmental appraisal programmes have not yet been strictly implemented.
>
> (Gou, 2010: 3–4)

In the midst of China's increasing state sponsorship of solar energy (Xinhua, 2009; Bradsher, 2009; Watts, 2009), the point of this book was hardly to portray China as the victim of Western exploitation, but was rather an attempted exposure of China's 'official view', in which the commitment to renewable energy was only a political façade of the same old development strategy (Delingpole, 2010). While national statistics on solar production rose, the silicon villages were left 'covered in grime and sweat' (Gou, 2010: 4). Thus, while the author condemned the hypocrisy of going green, he was equally critical of the Chinese government's blind self-congratulation and its ignorance in protecting the well-being of Chinese citizens.

This sentiment is captured on the very cover of *The Low Carbon Plot*, which asks two questions: 'Is low carbon a form of environmental protection or a new green politics? Is low carbon a political sacrifice resulting from great powers' gambling or is it a lifestyle ordinary citizens can look forward to?' The conflict inherent in these questions was not framed so much as China versus the West, or domestic versus international, but as institutional politics versus everyday quality of life. Here, the scepticism lies in terms of politicians' accountability to society. The book struck a chord in some segments of Chinese society as even though it was written for a domestic audience, *The Low Carbon Plot* is one of the few Chinese environmental books of which excerpts have been translated into English by Chinese netizens.[2]

However, climate sceptics are only one example of China's emerging public reflection over state–society relations and existing power structures. In recent years, environmental politics has become a topic that goes beyond the elite circle of policy makers and academics, into the realms of public debate (Tan and Zhou, 2005; Wang, 2005; Wei, 2007).

This is, in part, because the government's decisiveness in greening the state has failed to respond to everyday needs. In fact, Beijing's efforts seemed to have fallen into a familiar characterisation: Armed with tens of billions of RMB in loans from Chinese Development Bank and having comparable advantage of scale, China has, in the words of the *People's Daily*, 'employed powerful economic and policy instruments in implementing an environmental economy' and securing global market dominance (Lacey, 2011; Biggs, 2010; Zhong, 2012). Yet in the meantime, China's environment is still under threat, in part because of the structure of its energy

---

2 See <http://ourmaninsichuan.wordpress.com>.

supply. Renewable energy still makes up less than 10 per cent of China's energy consumption, with hydroelectric power, which raises ecological concerns of its own, being the main source (Qi, 2011: 289). China's ambition of becoming a world green energy leader can be traced back to 2007. According to Bloomberg Businessweek, Chinese officials were then 'deadly serious about investing in solar power capacity at home and eventually becoming a dominant player in this rapidly-emerging, clean energy technology' (Tschang, 2007). This 'deadly serious' level of decisiveness was for a number of reasons. For one, China's environment was already recognised as 'a world-class mess' and a growing embarrassment to the image of the country and government, especially in the lead-up to the 2008 Olympics (Tschang, 2007). For another, China's crude oil import dependence had been on the rise for years, which not only threatened national energy security in general but also, along with rising demand, contributed to fears over the economic impact of rolling blackouts which affected many small businesses in 2005 and again in 2008 (Xinhua, 2012b; Gou, 2010: 188–93).

For example, the 2005 oil and electricity shortage in the Pearl River delta and the month-long oil shortage in Guangdong in 2007 especially caught media attention.[3] One commentary which appeared in *Nanfang Daily* is an illustration of how the general public have started to demand further participation in political decisions. The author admitted that he was initially, as many Chinese, 'indifferent' about the energy crisis. As an ordinary salary earner, he was not interested in political participation and was used to the idea that the government would take care of such 'grand issues' as national energy security. But as the price of toys, IT products, transportation, medication and housing all went up, the author felt like a poor man with a high income. Feeling the pinch, his commentary highlighted the interrelatedness between political debate and everyday life, and ended with a strong urge for public action: 'for the big issues, can we still not care? Not worry? Not think of a response?' (Wang, 2005).

In summary, the core of Chinese green politics can be seen as an entangled negotiation of responsibilities. But the negotiations are not just between political institutions and bureaucrats. Increasingly, green politics in China is a discussion between the state and

---

3 See the dedicated Guangdong News webpages on the 2005 Pearl River delta oil shortage: <www.southcn.com/news/gdnews/zhzt/youhuang/>. And Xinhua News Press webpage on the 2007 Pearl River Delta oil shortage: <http://gd.xinhuanet.com/ztbd/youqi/>.

society. To comprehend how such negotiations have been made possible, it is necessary to first examine how Chinese perceive state–society relations and how a public questioning of authority has emerged.

China Is Not Happy

The Unhappy Government: What Entitles You to Lecture Me?

In pure statistics, there is much China should feel happy about in terms of its efforts to combat global climate change. Some see China as 'leading by action', pointing to its role in the CDM, where as mentioned in the Introduction, it can claim to be the source of more than half the world's Certified Emission Reductions (China Greentech Initiative, 2011; World Bank, 2009a: 262). But the raw numbers are even more impressive. In 2011, China led the world in renewable energy investment, responsible for almost one-fifth of total global investment at $52 billon (van der Slot and van den Berg, 2012). In addition, as a result of the 11th Five-Year Plan (from 2006 to 2010), China's energy intensity was reduced by 19.06 per cent. Finally, in comparison with studies in the United States and the United Kingdom, a 2009 national survey showed that the Chinese public demonstrate a better understanding of human-induced greenhouse gas (GHG) emissions (Duan, 2010: 5283).

But China is not happy. In fact, as this chapter shows, both the Chinese government and society have different things to worry about. For its part, Beijing is frustrated by a lack of recognition and the unfair pressure it feels is being put on China to commit to binding emission reductions. Chinese rage was on full display at the closing of the 2011 United Nations Climate Change Conference in Durban. Xie Zhenhua, head of the Chinese delegation, was agitated with the European Union for pressuring China to reach an agreement on its terms. Xie threw back the criticism with the piercing remark: 'What entitles you to lecture me here?'

A video clip from the Hong Kong Phoenix Satellite Television showed that this remark was proceeded with Xie berating his counterparts:[4] 'If we really want to react to climate change, then one must fulfil one's promises, take actions, make real contributions in achieving goals in relation to responding to climate change. But now,

---

4 See <http://news.ifeng.com/world/special/deban/content-3/detail 2011 12/11/11246538 0.shtml>.

there are certain countries, we are not looking at what you say, but what you do' (Yan and Lin, 2011).

Xie went on with a series of questions:

> These countries talked about a massive reduction of emissions – have they met these reductions? They talked about providing developing countries with financial and technical support – have they made such provisions? These promises have been talked for the last 20 years, but none have been fulfilled. We are developing countries, we need to develop, we need to eradicate poverty, we need to protect the environment, we've done all that we should have done. We have done what you have not. Then what entitles you to lecture me here?
>
> (Yan and Lin, 2011)

This was not the first time a Chinese delegation had become angry at a UN climate summit. In Copenhagen in 2009, Xie also made a similar rebuke to Western delegates, asking them 'What entitles you to negotiate with me?' This comment was also directed at the failed promises of technical and financial support from developed countries.

Clearly, China is not shy of displaying its discontent. According to *China Times*, the Chinese delegation's experience at Copenhagen can be summarised as 'the first day, unhappy; the second day, very unhappy; the third day, extremely unhappy' (Zhang, 2009). To some extent, Xie's first 'international rage' in 2009 was almost an enactment of the bestseller *Unhappy China: The great time, grand vision and our challenges*, published nine months prior to the Copenhagen summit (Song et al., 2009). *Unhappy China* was widely regarded as a follow-up version to the 1996 national bestseller *China Can Say No* (Zhang et al., 1996). Both books promoted a form of extreme nationalism, and seemed to embrace the idea that China was a rising power which could afford some attitude. *Unhappy China* argued that China has been too deferential to the West and that 'with Chinese national strength growing at an unprecedented rate, China should stop debasing itself and come to recognize the fact that it has the power to lead the world, and the necessity to break away from Western influence' in order to carve out its own position of pre-eminence' (Song et al., 2009).

As with the 'unhappy' episode in 2009, Xie's remark in 2011 made headlines in many Chinese news outlets, and the Durban video clip quickly became a hit among Chinese netizens. But similar to the *Unhappy* book which, despite its huge sales, failed to strike a chord amongst average Chinese with its narrow nationalism, Xie's speech received a mixed reaction within China (Wu, 2009). One example is from Ge Quan, contributing author to the reports of the Fourth and Fifth Assessments of the Intergovernmental Panel on Climate Change, who found Xie's speech indulging and ironic at the same time:

> Xie had a point and it was a point well made. Of course as a Chinese, I found that speech very indulging (*guoyin*). But then the irony is why wouldn't you communicate these ideas earlier? From what I know, [as a climatologist], actually China is one of the most active countries in the world pushing for a low-carbon transition. This is not just at the national level, but at the local level as well. There are provincial greenhouse gas emission monitors, provincial low-carbon initiatives, and so on. Even at urban district level, such as Chaoyang district in Beijing, efforts are being made. Why not make these things known to the world, so that others can understand your situation more? If one wants to be seen as following the rules and reason, then one should act like this from the start and in all aspects. But instead, at the very last meeting, the Chinese delegate throws in some angry and desperate remark. It wouldn't be wise for the image, would it? ... China is partly responsible for the existing bias against it as it still has to work on how to communicate and what to communicate with the world.

Ge is not alone in worrying about China's (lack of) communicative strategies. A major initiative of Beijing's has been to promote its image and enhance its own soft power in the face of international anxiety (Barr, 2011). Xie's outburst does not do much to help such efforts. 'To speak less and to act more' (*shaoshuo duogan*) has always been considered a virtue in Chinese culture, but it is perhaps more celebrated in modern history, as it embodies a pragmatic approach for an impoverished nation to strive for social progress without 'wasting' time and resources in endless argument or ideological fervour. But some Chinese are starting to question if such rationales have led to a neglect of the values of transparency and accountability. As Ge pointed out, 'If one wants to be seen as following the rules and reason, then one should act like this from the start.' Here, the term 'act' not only denotes the implementation of an agenda, but also refers to the act of explaining and communicating what measures have been taken.

Thus, Ge's worry about China's 'image-building' is not so much about whether China is 'likeable' in the eyes of others, but about whether China appears to be 'accountable' or 'to be seen as following the rules and reason'. Through his own participation in international climate dialogues, Ge acknowledged a reality of different views: 'Of course the West is biased when they view China. In fact, we Chinese may have similar bias against the West. I feel they always try to enforce their idea on us. They always think they must be right, and you must be wrong because of your political system.' But for Ge, simple nationalism or playing tough is not a solution to practical problems. After all, in his words, 'what's the point of having meetings if there is no meaningful dialogue but only bias?'

Ge was not alone in feeling anxious that China was not sending out the right message about improving its environmental record. Yan Qi, professor at Tsinghua University, said that in his research, 'We do not pay too much attention to people's "intention" or their "stands" on these issues. We care about what has happened and who can do what.' This pragmatic view was not limited to academia but is also strongly echoed by grassroots activists.

Teng Anyu, founder of an underground ENGO, said that she didn't need to follow 'the scientific arguments about climate change, because I *know* the environment is changing and it is changing in a bad direction' (original emphasis). Her certainty lies in her personal experience:

> I can feel it. Autumn should have been the best time in Beijing. But these days it's always foggy. The Birds Nest Olympic stadium is only a kilometre away from my apartment, but I cannot even see it from my window now because of the smog. Another thing that shocked me was in spring 2002, when Beijing was hit by a severe sandstorm. I was to test the white balance function of a new camera. I made many test shots, but every one of them came out yellow. The weather felt hopeless. So I do not doubt that we must do something about the environment and the way we live.

Views such as this illustrate a sense of anger, which is aggravated by a growing number of pollution cases and environmental accidents. Despite Beijing's attempts to control the flow of information online, such events are frequently communicated through social websites. In fact, just a few days before Xie's speech at the Durban 2011conference, many cities in the northern and eastern parts of China were confronted with impenetrable smog. During this time, at the Beijing Capital International Airport alone, 219 flights were cancelled and 118 were delayed. Similar problems hit transport networks across China, including as far north as Shandong and as far south as Fujian (Shan and Wang, 2011).

The urgency and intimacy of environmental vulnerability experienced by Chinese society is enough to cause distress. But as the next section shows, it is the reaction of Chinese authorities that makes people equally unhappy.

The Unhappy Society: Whom Should We Blame?

In the aftermath of Copenhagen and amid the 'unhappy China' discourse, the world saw two large oil spills. One took place in late spring 2010, in the Gulf of Mexico. During the three months of turmoil 4.9 million barrels of crude oil escaped into the ocean, leaving devastating ecological consequences, and causing significant economic loss to the coasts of Louisiana, Mississippi and Alabama. As a result British Petroleum's (BP's) chief executive, Tony Hayward, resigned, and the company indicated it would pay for the clean-up and remediation costs regardless of the statutory liability cap.

The second spill occurred in mid-July 2010, when two of the oil pipes belonging to Petro China exploded near China's northern harbour city Dalian. As a consequence more than 60,000 metric tons of crude oil spilled into the ocean (Stanway, 2010). Experts suggested the environmental consequences from the spill could last up to a decade.[5]

Similarly to the BP case, this oil spill also raised the question of environmental liability standards. According to Article 91 of China's Marine Environment Protection Law, liability is set at 30 per cent of direct economic loss, with a cap of 300,000 RMB, equal to approximately £30,000 (Ministry of Land and Resources, 1999). The initial rescue plan relied on taxpayers' money, as Petro China was reluctant to discuss the issue of compensation in public (Z. Li, 2010). Local fishermen were hired to clean up the spill with no special health or safety protections (Wang, 2010). A couple of leading news outlets, such as Netease and China Business News, simultaneously adopted the phrase 'people's war' (*renmin de*

---

5 See the dedicated news site: <http://news.sohu.com/s2010/youguan baozha/>.

zhandou) to capture the level of responsibility on the general public to control the effects of the spill[6] (Y. Li, 2010).

One of the news reports said:

> we saw the bodies of fire-fighters drowned in floating oil. Even though the dead were quickly given the honour of being called 'heroes', we are still exposed to the cruelty of the scene...Due to a lack of professional clean-up equipment, people were seen using their hands or plastic barrels in scooping up the oil. Some even used chopsticks.
>
> (Y. Li, 2010)

The news report highlighted one question: 'The Americans vent their anger at BP but whom should we blame?'

The Petro China spill is illustrative of a much larger and growing public frustration. In addition to anger over human-made disasters, China's vulnerability to natural events has seemingly increased because of a degrading environment and changing climate. According to official data released in July 2012, in the first half of that year alone, more than 113 million people in China had been affected by natural disasters, with 465 deaths, 97 missing and a direct economic cost of 77.38 billion RMB (China News, 2012). These numbers not only underline how expensive environmental vulnerability is, but also attach a human face to it. Public questioning of authority, at least on environmental issues, is an increasing phenomenon in China. We demonstrate this point in the next section by referring to two cases that happened in tandem in late summer 2012.

Public Questioning of Authority

The July 21, 2012 weather forecast in Beijing suggested rainstorms, but the capital was no stranger to heavy downpours in the summer. Thus most Beijingers carried on with their lives as normal. For example, one of our friends was planning to attend a concert in Wukesong, in west Beijing, that evening, and another friend was to drive back to his home from a holiday in Inner Mongolia. Neither one managed to make it to their destination. By late afternoon a flash flood hit Beijing with an intensity of rainfall that took everyone by surprise and paralysed the capital. According

---

6 See also photo reportage, <http://news.163.com/photoview/3R710001/ 10169.html#p=6CKGAF023R710001>.

to statistics later published by the People's Daily Online, 56,933 people had to be evacuated and 79 people died. Traffic came to a halt in places in and around the capital as people abandoned their vehicles. The underground and airport were also affected, and 229 flights cancelled and 246 flights were delayed at Beijing Capital International Airport.[7]

While parts of Beijing were submerged in water and rescue was underway, the internet in China was enduring another kind of flood, with the public demanding answers.

Questions were raised on a long list of issues, including the efficiency of the weather warning system, the competence of the meteorology office, the municipality resilience schemes, the transparency of data, including death tolls, public spending and quality control on infrastructures, and the suitability of contingency plans in public buildings and offices (Rao and Jin, 2012; Jinghua Times, 2012). As the Associate Press noted:

> The city has seen tens of billions of dollars poured into its modernization, adding iconic venues for the 2008 Olympics, the world's second-largest airport, new subway lines and dazzling skyscrapers – all while basics like water drainage were apparently neglected. Many were left wondering how badly prepared other less-prosperous parts of China must be.
>
> (Olsesen, 2012)

As questions and criticism rose, a local downpour became an international embarrassment for China. With pressure from both domestic and international media, the People's Daily Online created a special page hosting a collection of news and data regarding the deluge. Its content was also simultaneously translated into English, Russian, French, Arabic and Spanish.

The intensity of public questioning of the authorities can be seen from the fact that people did not easily accept the government's response. One example was that warnings about the coming storm relied on traditional media such as television and radio, while only 7 per cent of randomly selected Beijing residents received a text alert (Jin et al., 2012). While this might seem high to some, we must remember that in China mobile phone culture is dominant. As of 2012, there were over one billion users (Xinhua, 2012a). In the aftermath of the event, netizens argued that much loss could have been avoided if modern communication channels had been better

---

7 <www.english.people.com.cn>.

employed (Jiang et al., 2012). According to *Beijing News*, the deputy director of the Beijing Metrological Bureau, Qu Xiaobo, reportedly dismissed this suggestion, saying it was beyond the network capacity to contact Beijing's 20 million residents (Rao and Jin, 2012). In a separate interview, the head of the Beijing Metrological Station also confirmed that 7 per cent was the maximum capacity (Chen and Wang, 2012). But this excuse was further questioned by mobile network experts. They claimed that the capacity for a mass distribution of information through Chinese mobile networks was between 10,000 to 100,000 messages per second, and that the networks had sustained similar flows of texting in periods such as the Spring Festival (Jin et al., 2012; Wu, 2012).

In this case, public scrutiny of the authorities yielded some result. On September 1, 2012, when another rainstorm was forecast in Beijing, the Beijing Met Office, in collaboration with China Mobile, China Unicom and China Telecom, sent warning messages to Beijing residents (Jin, 2012a).

The public persistence in querying authority is not limited to high-profile cases such as the Beijing rainstorm, but is also shown in local disputes. Only two weeks later, on August 12, 2012, another environmental distress hit the headlines: fish farmers in Anxin County in Baiyangdian found a noxious smell coming from their local river. Within three days, despite oxygen pumps and medications, all of their fish were found to be dead. It was estimated that the local fisheries suffered about 10 million RMB losses. The location of this incident, in the Baiyangdian area of the county, is a famous wetland resort 160 km south of Beijing. Its natural beauty has inspired a collection of Chinese modern literature known for its romanticism and simple and delightful prose. The body of writing even takes its name from the area, as it is called the Baiyangdian school. However, this famous wetland and source of poetic imagination is now spoiled with stench and piles of dead fish. After the event, the local government had to send a dredge boat and an excavator to help clean up the river. Experts and professionals from both the county and city were sent to the site to analyse water samples.

According to an official statement by the Anxin County government, the incident was the result of an over-population of fish as a result of excessive farming, in combination with a seasonal floods and the earlier July 21 record rainfall in nearby Beijing (Wang and Luo, 2012; Zhang and Meng, 2012). The sudden increase of water was said to have stirred up the mud, fish feed residuals, and excrements from the river bed, which decreased the oxygen level in the water. This made the already over-populated water incapable of sustaining the fish. In other words, according to the authorities, this was an unfortunate accident caused by minor operational fault on the part of local fish farmers. The process of loss claims with the local authority had already started and a compensation scheme was said to be underway to help the fish farmers resume work.

However, the fish farmers in Anxin did not buy this explanation. They claimed years of fish farming experience and knew their ponds well. They suspected that the real cause of the incident was illegal dumping by upstream textile mills and leather factories. For one thing, farmers had tried pumping oxygen into the river but this was to no avail. For another, witnesses said that the river was discoloured and had a strange smell during the affected time period. So in the farmers' view, the reason could not have been a simple overflow of water. In fact, similar though smaller events had plagued nearby regions in 2006 and 2000 (Gao, 2006; Wang, 2006). In both cases, the water returned to normal after the government closed down nearby factories. While this time the authorities denied water pollution, the farmers indicated that they were going to start an investigation of their own, and if sufficient evidence was collected, they would take legal action against those responsible (Zhang and Meng, 2012).

Our examples in this chapter show that while the world sees a wealthier, stronger and more easily agitated 'China' at the global negotiation table, we should not forget its people are also becoming more vocal, making more demands, and pursuing more means to fulfil those demands. In understanding a country that is commonly described as authoritarian, it is easy, even tempting, to forget that state and society constitute both sides of the same unhappy China. However, as development studies specialist Peter Ho rightly observed, in China:

> repression is a reality; this does not mean, however that the People's Republic can be labelled an authoritarian state with no space for dissenting voices or voluntary organisation. Such a label would overlook the many strategies that citizens can employ to escape from the government's control, and would fail to uncover the complex patters of interaction between state and society that shape environmental movements.
>
> (Ho, 2001: 897)

The Chinese public no longer take authorities for granted. When their daily lives start to be affected, they ask questions and are persistent in getting a credible answer. It's not simply a blame game or to pass the buck to others, but they want to hold the authorities accountable for what they have claimed to do. They do not settle for perfunctory explanations (for example text message capacity), nor are they easily appeased by clumsy cover-ups (for example the claim that there was not enough oxygen in the pond). They exercise their rights as taxpayers in questioning the public infrastructure, as well as the appropriateness of contingency plans and warning systems. The cases in this section are hardly revolutionary, but the questions they raise send a powerful message to those who claim to speak for the people of China.

Conclusion

The first decade of the new millennium found China an unhappy emerging power. Whereas the government is increasingly confident in confronting Western criticism, it is only just beginning to learn how to handle domestic queries regarding its own use of power. Beijing may have some success in shrugging off Western intervention, but in some ways this only encourages the Chinese public to be more vocal in their calls for accountability from political institutions.

Much observation and guesswork have been devoted to deciphering the government's logic and projecting its next move. Is China a revisionist power or a status-quo player? Is it a reckless polluter or a responsible environmental leader? In 1994, Sprinz and Vaahtoranta established an interest-based explanation of countries' support for international environmental policy. According to this research, four types of attitudes can be identified on basis of 'ecological vulnerability' and 'abatement costs'. The four categories are bystanders, draggers, pushers and intermediates. 'Bystanders' refer to regions where both ecological vulnerability and abatement costs are low. 'Pushers' are those with high vulnerability but low costs. China, with its high vulnerability and high abatement costs, falls into the category of intermediates.

But a simple classification of a whole country is hardly helpful in shedding light on its environmental situation. In the past two decades, China has perhaps remained an 'intermediate' player. However, much has changed within China. Both the Chinese government and society are displeased with the environmental liabilities that are projected onto them.

From the state's perspective, Xie Zhenhua's fury at the UN climate summit can be seen as a protest against an almost 'habitual' blame of developing countries. Xie's speech is one of many government attempts to break the usual divide in roles between the North and South which is implied in international discourse. However, development interests and power relations are much more entangled than a simple North/South binary can account for. While China remains a key mediator between the developed and developing countries, it has its own image problem to deal with and its own environment responsibilities to reflect on.

Climatologist Ge Quan, who participated in early climate negotiations, noted a change in China's negotiation strategy:

> At the very beginning, in international negotiations, China emphasized average emissions per capita. We knew then that 'average' is the killer word. But gradually, we have started to avoid mentioning emissions per person, because we have already reached the world average and our total has increased as well. These are matters of fact.

In addition, China is not purely an 'exploited South' either. We noted earlier how developed countries dislocate their environmental burden by consuming goods produced in China. Increasingly, China is doing the same by exploiting resources in other countries. Africa is the example most often cited, but examples closer to China include wildlife trade for medical usage and illegal timber imports from Indonesia and Burma (Hamlin, 2009; Zbicz, 2009). Green politics, then, is not just a balance of the accounts, but also a balance of accountabilities.

It should be clear that Chinese citizens are dissatisfied at the ill-matched image of a 'rising nation' with the experience of incompetent governance at home. In the face of rainstorms or illegal dumping, they have found no one to be held accountable but were instead left fighting a 'people's war'. The contrast with other countries with more open systems further leads to the demand for institutions to take up their fair share of social liabilities. As in shown in both the cases of the Beijing rains and Baiyangdian, the Chinese public are not quieted by easy answers, but push for a response until it meets their expectations. This is not just an awakening to the responsibility of the state or a call for a bigger government. It is, as is further demonstrated in Chapters 2 and 3, also an awakening to their own responsibilities, such as their duties to monitor authority, to exercise their legal rights, to participate in public affairs, and to struggle for a fairer society.

Environment dialogues are renegotiations of responsibilities. It is this recognition of responsibilities that forms the basis of action. In an entangled global web of interests and needs, it may be difficult to pin down who should be blamed for environmental risks. The answers may be multiple and all equally valid. But it is through a continuous attempt to better answer this question that many stakeholders have pushed for legal and social reforms. For people living in China, environmental risks necessitate taking general precautions on a daily basis.

2 WAYS OF SEEING

In discussing the environment, it is easy to make several assumptions. For example, it might seem obvious that given a choice, most people would resist living in a polluted environment and would seek a long healthy life. If such a consensus could be established, it could serve as a rational foundation for future agreements and collaborative goals. It would then be logical to conclude that to go green simply requires the enlightening of opportunist polluters blinded by short-term benefits. Yet it is easy to forget that conscious tolerance of pollution and understandings of the good life may vary dramatically in different contexts. Thus, what first needs to be illuminated is not what ought to be done, but how people make sense of their reality and their options.

For example, China's air pollution is not a recent occurrence, but it is only in recent years that it has been recognised as a problem by an increasing number of Chinese. Even in the late 1990s, people living in Beijing rarely enjoyed a blue-sky day. One of the authors, Zhang, spent a good portion of those years commuting daily by bicycle between the Chaoyang and Dongcheng districts. The 20-minute ride always ended with her having watery and itchy eyes. On one particular day in 1998 Zhang remembers how a spring rain washed the sky clean. But what struck her was that after the rain stopped and water evaporated, all the bikes parked in the open air were covered in a thick layer of grey dirt, reminding her of the seabed relics from the movie *Titanic* which she had just watched. Although she didn't require an expert to tell her, or anyone else living in Beijing at the time, that the city's air was heavily polluted, like most Beijingers in the 1990s she never thought of it as a problem. In fact, on occasions when Zhang's overseas relatives visited China and complained about the air quality, she always found their complaints puzzling: 'Sure, the air in China is not as clean as in the West, but why does it matter?' The economy was booming, life quality was improving, world culture and global fashion were filling the streets, and everyone seemed to be getting on happily. Like many city dwellers at the time, Zhang knew the poor air quality was an 'issue', but she was more concerned about Beijing becoming an international city.

A similar, and perhaps more telling, example comes from Su Gaopeng, an environmental photographer. During one of his trips to a remote Chinese village in the late 1990s, he immediately fell in love with the village's natural beauty. Su described it as resembling a classic Chinese painting: vast fields, light grey mountains in the background, a winding narrow country path and small sheds in the foreground. He pointed out this sight to his host and commented with admiration, 'This is such a pretty scene.' His host, a local farmer, was genuinely baffled. He turned around, pointing to the other direction, where two tall chimneys of a newly built factory were puffing out white smoke. 'See that white smoke? It is like we are manufacturing white clouds in the sky. That is a pretty scene. We are proud of it.'

It is unlikely that anyone would interpret these two cases as evidence that Beijing dwellers or Chinese farmers prefer to live with pollution. Rather, these examples demonstrate situations in which pollution was tolerated by local residents as a reasonable cost, given the rewards. More than a decade later, both air pollution and factory waste have attracted much public debate within China, as we discuss in Chapter 3. To some extent, it is true to say that pollution has long been a part of public life in China, but it is only in recent years that the public has started to see it as reason to worry. The problematisation of pollution itself is a process in which ordinary citizens (for example urban residents or rural farmers) attempt to make sense of the immediate social milieu in which they are situated, and to identify what, if anything, they ought to do. To borrow a concept from the sociologist Pierre Bourdieu, it is this social habitus that both forms the basis of perception of social experience, and generates practice (Bourdieu, 1980[1990]: 52–65). Bourdieu uses the term habitus to refer to the lifestyle, values and expectations of particular social groups that are acquired through the activities and experiences of everyday life.

Thus, to properly assess China's green activism, it is necessary to have a good grasp of the social habitus at work. That is, we need to understand, first, how Chinese activists interpret their relationships and integrate those with their expectations for environmental action, and second, how they act upon their values to affect change through viable channels of participation. While Chapter 3 is focused on the latter point, this chapter investigates the former.

Three examples will be examined in turn. They are ENGO-led

natural photography events, the emergence of bird-watching societies and a recent grassroots protest against commercial interests. These examples may not be representative but they are indicative of the social milieu of China's green politics. Public engagement events, such as bird watching and photography, are often characterised as non-political and are criticised as being 'safe' in that they evade confrontations with authority (Lee, 2003; Schwartz, 2004; Feng, 2009). However, we argue that the popularity of these two activities sheds light on how ordinary Chinese perceive their social-ecological habitus, which formulates and justifies their priorities and strategies in green activism. Similarly, as in the grassroots protest example discussed in this chapter, we recognise that bottom-up initiatives in China are constrained by their lack of political and financial leverage (Economy, 2005; Ho and Edmonds, 2008). But it is useful to be reminded that in a largely authoritarian country, the presentation of a public gaze is itself an act of resistance, a form of organised action. Social actors operate according to certain pictures they have of the world. By examining what Chinese actors have found by looking through camera lenses and telescopes, this chapter is not simply exhibiting different ways of seeing the environment. Rather, it is only through understanding the scenes actors associate themselves with that we can we start to comprehend their behaviour within them.

Looking Through the Lens

Visual representations have increasingly gained importance in environmental politics. A single photograph of a natural disaster or endangered wildlife is often more powerful than words in invoking sympathy and a shared sense of responsibility among an otherwise disengaged public (Lowe et al., 2006; Smith and Joffe, 2009; DiFrancesco and Young, 2011). Beyond institutional campaigns and media coverage, ENGOs too are not shy in adhering to this general trend in the 'aestheticization of contemporary politics' (Papastergiadis, 2012). With selective and calculative framings, visual representations of environmental issues are often seen as an effective way to influence public discourse and governance conventions (Entman, 1993; Boykoff, 2011).

Photography and videos are also widely employed by Chinese ENGOs of various sizes and geographic locations. However, in the Chinese context, photography and film go well beyond a form of objectification or voyeurism in which the photographer is freed from responsibility and unable to intervene (Sontag, 1977). In fact, as is demonstrated in this section, the sociopolitical influence of visual representations is achieved not only through the exhibition of photos, but also through the making of them. The public, instead of merely being the recipients of professional images, are encouraged and assisted by Chinese ENGOs in holding up their lenses and observing nature through their own viewfinders.

A key strategy of ENGOs is to offer free weekend natural photography classes and low-budget field trips. Most of these classes are often jointly taught by photographers and related natural science professionals, providing practical knowledge and hands-on tutoring. As such, these events incentivise participants' own examinations of human–nature relations.

There are at least three features of Chinese ENGOs' organisation of photographic classes that seem to indicate a different approach in promoting collective action. First, the limelight is on the action of the general public, who have little or no previous knowledge of photography. Through offering free natural photography classes, the primary aim of Chinese ENGOs is to expand their presence and influence to wider social circles, so as to get more people engaged with local environmental issues. To be sure, most of these amateur photographs are for private consumption. Only a small percentage will ever be exhibited in public or shared online. Even when they are, the audience is usually small and the influence normally remains local. Thus a second feature is that the intended impact lies not in the aesthetic value of the resulting work, but in the individualised process of observation, questioning and conscious framing of nature and its relation to everyday life. With China's progressive urbanisation, several green activists interviewed expressed concerns about people's increasing alienation from the natural environment, especially Chinese city dwellers. 'You can't protect nature unless you know what nature is', was a common rationale underlying most image courses organised by ENGOs. Thus, to some extent Chinese ENGOs are using camera lenses to turn onlookers into 'witnesses' of human relations with nature (DiFrancesco and Young, 2011: 531).

Third, although it is hard to quantify their impact, it would be a mistake to overlook the normative implications of these loosely organised photographic events. Of the nine ENGOs we visited with diverse priorities (for example wildlife protection, desertification, water pollution, industry pollution), five organise natural photography classes as a specific form of public engagement.

This proportion may not be representative, but it is indicative of how natural photography is starting to gain popularity with ENGOs as a form of public interface in steering collective behaviour at the grassroots level. China's experience seems to demonstrate that the contemporary dynamics between art and politics goes beyond a linear understanding of 'either the pictorial representation of political messages, or the political inspiration that is drawn *from* art'. Rather, the importance lies in 'the transformation that occurs *through* the interplay between the creative imagination and inter-subjective relations' (Papastergiadis, 2012: 135, original emphasis).

Making It Real: Encouraging the Public's Will to Act

There are manifold ways in which images help to promote the public understanding of environmental challenges in China. For example, images can function as vehicles transmitting otherwise distant situations to the public. This is the case for one of the most well-known Chinese environmental groups, Wild China Films, an agency that is dedicated to the visual documentation of Chinese wildlife and human–nature relations, as well as for the Kekexili volunteer network, which organised a photographic tour through nearly 100 universities in China to raise awareness of environmental degradation and illegal mining in Tibet (Huang, 2008). Photographs may also be used as evidence in monitoring policy implementations. For example, a number of ENGOs, most notably the Da'erwen Natural Knowledge Club (*Da'erwen Ziran Qiuzhi She*), use Weibo (the Chinese equivalent of Twitter) to publicise water pollution photos along with related data in order to help spread awareness of possible violations. Visual images are also used in giving a narrative to an idea. One ENGO we visited focuses on desertification, and employs documentary films of southwestern Chinese rural traditions to communicate the idea of 'sustainable agriculture'. In another case, a student association based in Lanzhou aired its documentary film on village life in a national conservation area through provincial television stations to give a human perspective on the balance between environmental conservation and social development.

However, these examples do not form our primary concern. Such conventional uses of natural images may have helped to increase general knowledge of environmental problems. Yet despite a relatively high level of public concern for China's growing environmental crisis, a key challenge remains a lack of long-term participation. In fact, nation-wide surveys highlight that the majority of the Chinese surveyed disassociate these problems with their personal actions and consider them a responsibility of national institutions (Wang, 2008: 95–111; Hong, 2007). For many green activists, this alienation of individual environmental responsibilities presents a serious impediment in making improvements on the ground. As explained by Wang Shuo, an activist in Beijing:

> it's true that something must be done through institutional channels. But if everyone thinks environmental protection is irrelevant to their daily routines as individual citizens, then there is no real incentive for the government to deal with it either. Only when the public reckon something is close to their interests, would government or industries then be motivated to handle it.

In other words, the key challenge is how to motivate the public in connecting their own role with environmental protection. One of the strategies ENGOs developed in changing this situation was employing natural photography. Teng Anyu, who left a high-profile ENGO and founded her own underground ENGO in Beijing, explained her rationale as follows:

> My previous experience in working with big-name NGOs reached the point where I realised there is little use in just talking within the comfortable circle of like-minded environmental activists. You have to get those indifferent people involved too .... I was so touched and inspired by a Taiwan organization, the Society of Wilderness's attentiveness to influencing ordinary people and making small changes in basic everyday chores. Then I thought, why can't we have an organisation that is perhaps not so professionally high-end, but can get more public involved? ... So my friends and I started our own organisation using image and image-making as a way to get common people interested.

Most green activists we interviewed echoed Teng Anyu's view that Chinese ENGOs need to be creative in getting 'indifferent people' engaged and to ground the big picture of environmental protection in 'everyday' life, so as to make it intelligible and do-able for the public. It is likely not a coincidence that the making of natural photography appeared to be a good choice in reaching out to otherwise uninterested individuals. For one thing, the intense popularity of photographic gadgets in China (for example cameras, cell phones, digital video recorders) provides fertile ground for image-minded ENGOs to build upon. In addition, while public environmental education may sound daunting and boring to many, learning how to manipulate a camera successfully and photograph outdoors holds great appeal to a diversity of people, especially students and the middle class. One of Teng's colleague, Xiao Wangzi, regarded this as simply environmental communication keeping pace with society: 'we must admit that we live in a digital age ... digital cameras and digital recorders are no longer a luxury for a great number of people. Photography provides a reasonable opportunity and an acceptable method for most people to get to know nature.'

One dominant form of incorporating natural photography into environmental programmes is hosting free lessons with follow-up photographic field trips. The authors attended one such class in Beijing, and complemented this experience with other interviewees' accounts. These events can be briefly described as follows. Almost all these lessons are half- to one-day free public events organised over the weekend. Anyone of any age group and educational background can join in. The events are normally advertised through organisational websites, online forums, micro-blogs and text messages. Photographic themes often rotate between a diversity of subjects, such as birds, flowers, insects, trees, water, stars and even frogs. The idea is to maximise the potential audience since, in the words of Teng, 'as long as someone is interested in any one of these subjects, they can come and listen to our talks'. The invited tutors consist mostly of photographers, magazine editors and academic researchers, who share their knowledge on the natural phenomena under discussion and on related photographic techniques. These classes often later have follow-up field trips in which photographic exercises are combined with observing wildlife.

Offering free photography lessons has proved to be an effective way of getting the wider public engaged with environmental issues. For example, although the Chinese government's tight restrictions on civil group registration have forced Teng Anyu's organisation (mentioned above) to remain in the legal grey area of an underground ENGO, it is nonetheless able to host around 50 natural photographic events every year. In fact it often needs to put a cap on its events because of the high volume of people signing up. In the past four years, this ENGO has grown from only a handful of members to almost 2,000. Another example is the programmes hosted by the Nature University in collaboration with several leading Chinese ENGOs. The aim of these programmes is to enable everyone to be a 'citizen environmental protection expert' (*gongmin huanbao zhuanjia*). They provide public lectures on a variety of subjects, of which natural photography is one. According to the website, the natural photography series started in 2008, and 'experience proved that this [natural photography] is a topic of special appeal to many'.[1]

As most of the Nature University's events are open to all, the seminars are usually set at an introductory level. For example, one advertisement reads, 'there is no restrictions on participants, no fee required. People with or without cameras or previous knowledge on photography are all welcome'.[2] Song Gaopeng, volunteer instructor for a couple of ENGOs, noted these sessions were mainly about getting ordinary people inside environmental circles and feeling at home:

> Information such as a plant's taxonomy or surviving popula-
> tion is of interest to academics, but means very little to ordinary
> people, who may be more curious about how they live, where
> they live, can we see where they live .... Although it's superficial,
> we are happy to maintain it that way. For example, we never
> organise photography trips to conservation areas. We always take
> people to suburbs where ordinary people have access because we
> want to give our participants a way that they can observe and
> experience nature by themselves.

As with Teng Anyu, Song Gaopeng's view on these public classes is not oriented at 'professionally high-end' people. In this way, Chinese ENGOs have clearly embraced the stance that there is a need to 'break out of the environmental ghetto' and to transform the topic into an 'all of society' problem rather than an elite concern (Hall and Taplin, 2007). Clear and accessible material is favoured over dense statistics or expensive wildlife explorations. For this, as explained by Song, gives participants something 'to observe and experience by themselves'. It is obvious that these photographic lessons are aimed not primarily at producing stunning art, but at relating environmental facts in the context of an individual pastime. To be sure, we could attribute this phenomenon to the cultural context. Asians, perhaps especially Chinese, are often seen as fond of photography. They are seen posing and zooming in and out at 'scenic spots' and social gatherings to 'preserve memories' (*liuying/liunian*). This photophilic culture creates an opportunity for ENGOs.

Learning how to photograph nature creates a symbolic connection between city dwellers and the natural environment. This is important,

---

1 See <www.bjep.org.cn>.
2 See <www.bjep.org.cn/index4.asp?linkto=c39&cmenu=700>.

as one major challenge in instigating long-term public commitment in China is to connect environmental problems with an individual's will to act. In responding to this situation, some Chinese ENGOs see encouraging the public to create their own images as a way to generate personal interest in the natural world. In the next section we discuss how camera lenses incentivise an otherwise indifferent public to help with environmental causes.

Recasting Individual Responsibility Through the Lens

Several activists interviewed suggested a subtle difference between the impact of an image and the impact of *making* an image. This highlights a unique value of encouraging more people to hold up their camera lenses. One example is from Fan Xiaoxi, a Shanghai environmental volunteer. Fan remarked on the importance of visual presentations in shaping environmental awareness by drawing on the comparison that 'most people in China may be familiar with wild animals in Africa or the North Pole through TV programmes, but they know nothing about endangered wild life in China'. But he further added, for the purpose of environmental protection, the power of visual images is not embedded in the pixels themselves, but in the human–nature relation they invoke. 'The point of photography is not really how pretty these animals and sceneries are,' said Fan, 'but how it [nature] connects to the local, how it connects to us and how its destiny may be connected to our destiny as human beings.' With this pragmatic concern of making people aware of nature's connection with themselves, photography, in addition to photographs, is seen as a tool in creating an engaged public. During a public outreach event co-organised with the Shanshui Association, this interviewee and his colleagues handed out simple point-and-shoot cameras to villagers and students, and encouraged them to record their lives and surroundings. Later, a small exhibition was organised in the same county to which both the photographers (that is, the villagers and students) and their families and friends came to see the work. When asked how these amateur photographs would promote environmental causes, Fan responded:

> The participants found it interesting, because when you are capturing things with lenses rather than bare eyes, you are no longer taking what you see for granted .... Perhaps to look with your eyes may be an act of unconsciousness, but once you have a medium or a tool to help you see, especially when you realise you can share your view with others, you may frame your values,

judgements and ideas within that view. So you are more cognisant of what you perceive.

For Fan, a camera lens is 'a medium' or 'a tool' that enables ordinary people to be 'more cognisant' of the environment. Putting an individual behind a viewfinder, rather than in front of a ready-made picture, forces them into an open-ended dialogue with the object. They are led to contemplate not only what can be seen but also how possible perspectives should be incorporated (or not). A viewer of a picture or a listener to a statement might take its content for granted. Yet framing is never an act of 'unconsciousness', but creates an occasion to deliberate on and make salient the notion of self–other (in this case, self–nature) dynamics (Entman, 1993; Papastergiadis, 2012).

The reconceptualisation of human–nature relations seems to be of special importance in light of rapid urbanization and development in China. Wang Shuo started his environmental protection journey by working with staff members on national natural reserve (NNR) sites, but later switched to volunteering to host natural photographic seminars for several ENGOs including the China Green Student Forum. The point, as he saw it, was to use cameras to get ordinary people back in touch with nature:

> City dwellers, especially the young generation, now have very little chance to know about nature. They are instead surrounded by modern 'concrete forests'. The closest nature they can get their hands on is a park, with cleanly cultivated grass and few insects. They do not have any bond with nature. If you suggest we should cut down the tree to make paper, they'd say so what, go ahead. Because they are not aware of any 'functions' of the trees besides being turned into paper or furniture. But suppose they know about the tree and how many kinds of wild life survive on this tree, then they might be more conscious of a choice: is it necessary to cut it down, must the paper must be made, are there alternative ways?

As put forward by Wang, camera lenses provide a conduit for city dwellers to know nature not as simply a means of producing paper and furniture, but as indispensable to more integrated ends. It is not just about making prints of nature. It is about the making of nature's imprints on an individual.

Similar points are echoed in the comments of an IT technician,

Huo Jian, who has volunteered to provide web maintenance services to civic groups, and also participated in photographic seminars. He points out a potentially normative function of these seminars as 'seed[ing] a notion':

> Once we appreciate something, we normally hope it can be preserved, then the other deeper causes follow .... These photographic events hosted by ENGOs are not to instruct people what they ought to do, but rather to seed a notion in them. Once you have found its [nature's] beauty and maybe one day it may disappear, then you start to think of what actions to take yourself. If an increasing number of people walk in to these classes and to nature, one day it may grow from personal appreciation to a public need. Then what people ask for may not be buying a house or buying cars, but to require a piece of green beside the buildings .... Anyway, we need to find and address the most fundamental issue in people's hearts, for there lies the ultimate answer to the environmental problem.

A fundamental solution to environmental challenges, as Huo Jian suggests, is to 'seed a notion' in people's inner aspirations. It may be difficult to pinpoint what exactly this notion is, other than a recasting of individual responsibility. The experience of Chinese environmental groups seems to further expand such idea. This is to say, by encouraging more people to view the environment through lenses, the intended reflection goes beyond the relationship between self and other humans, but includes (re)cognition of the relationship between self and nature.

New Forms of Mobilization

As we mentioned previously, an increasingly influential way of understanding China's approach to environmental policy making is the theory of 'authoritarian environmentalism', which 'concentrates authority in a few executive agencies manned by capable and uncorrupt elites seeking to improve environmental outcomes' (Gilley, 2012: 288). We would not necessarily disagree with this characterisation. Nor do we wish to underplay the difficulties of successful policy implementation within a fragmented system. Our argument is a modest one, in that we do not wish to advocate either democratic or authoritarian environmentalism. We do, however, believe it is worth remembering that even authoritarian states require the mobilisation of social actors. Our book provides a novel example of how ENGOs are seeking to do this.

It is difficult, if not impossible, to quantify the actual influence of these natural photography events in promoting environmental protection in China. What is certain, however, is that camera lenses and natural images are regarded by many Chinese ENGOs as an effective channel to draw people closer to green initiatives. For the ENGO staff interviewed, offering photographic lessons and enabling more people to operate a viewfinder have at least two interrelated functions.

First, offering natural photographic tutoring is primarily seen by respondents as a way to gain a wider audience and potentially nurture greater public responsibility. Previously we discussed Tang Peng, founder of a leading green educational organisation in Beijing. Tang was among the first to incorporate photography into his public engagement agenda, and was also an active campaigner to transform indifferent onlookers into environmental actors. In Tang's view, there are social resources that are in deep sleep in China. It is the job of ENGOs to utilise these resources and in the process, expand their influence within the 'social biological system'. Thus, the main challenge to Chinese environmental protection is not an absence of resources, but rather the need to wake up social energies and turn them into a force to solve actual problems. In this context, photography emerged as a practical tool to interact with the wider 'social biological system'.

There are two points that should be highlighted about this first form of Chinese ENGOs' efforts to assimilate ordinary people into forces of environmental action. First, natural photography is only one of a combination of methods employed by Chinese ENGOs in assimilating social resources. Thus, as pointed out earlier, it is perhaps in vain to single out the sole impact of natural photography on Chinese green initiatives. However, the fact that natural photographic lessons and field trips are as common activities as dispensing recyclable bags, animal protection campaigns, garbage sorting and tree planting suggests that photography is at least an empirically satisfactory method embraced by many Chinese ENGOs. Second, China is not unique in employing photography to promote social change. It belongs to a long tradition of building social solidarities through artistic means.[3] However, the experience

---

3 See for example the cross-border organisation Collective Lens: <www. collectivelens.com>.

of Chinese ENGOs furthers our understanding of how potential social actors can be enticed at the grassroots level, and what forms of interventionist strategy can be employed in shaping collective behaviour (Touraine, 1988, 2000). One main characteristic of natural photographic events in China is that they do not only imply a linear monologue in which artists or experts exhibit their 'superior' or 'accredited' views with the aim to create 'an informed and concerned audience' (Kay, 2011: 424). Rather, in the present Chinese context, natural photographic events put as much emphasis, if not more, on the making of natural images by ordinary people. To some extent, it could be argued that Chinese ENGOs obliterate the linear presenter–receiver dynamic of environmental images. Most of the amateur photographs are for private consumption. The will to act is formed through an individual's own interface with nature and the framing of their own view. The importance of looking through the lenses lies in its ability to direct a recursive internal inspection of human–nature relations. This leads to the second function.

A second function of this photographic approach is that it provides a medium that reconnects humans with nonhumans. This may be of special social significance to China, a country that declared 'war on nature' half a century ago and has experienced rapid urban expansion over the last thirty years. One simple example, as given by Huo Jian, is that instead of yearning for bigger houses or faster cars, collective reorientation of human–nature relations could lead to prioritising campaigning for 'a piece of green' in the community. Like Huo, many green activists involved in the organisation and delivery of these natural photographic events emphasised how such activities help ordinary people to discover beauty in nature, and how empathy with nature's qualities may in turn impel actors to be 'more cognisant' (Fan Xiaoxi), 'start to think' (Huo Jian) or seek 'alternative ways' (Wang Shuo). At least in the eyes of green activists interviewed, subjectification starts with the self, but does not end with the self. Personal preference may lead to recognition of collective needs, which may be a source of social change.

More specifically, it is the making of natural images, rather than the mere exhibition of them, that seems to play a distinctive role in promoting environmental awareness in China. As such, natural imagery is not merely treated as a way to reduce complexity so as to make natural challenges 'consumable' for the general public (DiFrancesco and Young, 2011). Nor is the image itself considered adequate to 'bring the issue closer to home' to engender social commitments to environmental protection (Smith and Joffe, 2009:

658). Rather, the Chinese public are taught to take their own natural images. They are both producers and consumers of the images that may make them see differently. Visual tools, especially cameras, serve not only as an invitation to draw an otherwise indifferent public into the lecture rooms of ENGOs, but also as a conduit to recast the individual–environment relationship, which in turn may cultivate a more observant, accountable and reflective wider public.

An Alternative View of Public Engagement

Chinese ENGOs are both known for their public engagement and criticised by observers for it. The natural photography lessons analysed in the previous section are only one of a collection of new public engagement activities commonly referred to by ENGOs as 'ziran tiyan' (natural experience events). Other events in this category also aim at raising public awareness of human–nature relations, through for example camping, bird watching, weekend outings and family-oriented gardening workshops. However, this attention to working with the public (rather than with the authorities) has been interpreted by many as a sign of weakness in Chinese ENGOs, for these initiatives resemble environmental 'education' rather than confrontational 'actions' of the kind often seen in Western ENGOs (Schwartz, 2004; Lu, 2007; Tang and Zhan, 2008). The underlying rationale is that as long as China remains a one-party state, it is the government that remains the main mover for environmental progress. Thus, public education and self-reflective events generate little political impact and guarantee little social change. Until recent years, grassroots green activism in China has been ridiculed as specialising in only three peripheral issues: tree planting, bird watching and garbage collecting (zhishu, guanniao, jian laji) (Lu, 2007; Xu and Wan, 2008; Feng, 2009).

However, we argue for an alternative view: that public outreach and educational programmes organised by Chinese ENGOs are valuable actions with political significance. As a number of environmental scholars have rightly pointed out, in order to understand how the rise of ENGOs has brought change to state–society relations, we need to replace an institutional lens with that of the actors (Yang, 2005; Gui, Ma and Muhlhahn, 2009). In other words, instead of using government relations as a default benchmark in judging the success and failure of ENGOs in China, it is necessary to turn the examination of green activism back on itself. We need to come out of the conceptual box that contains state relations, and comprehend social behaviours in context. Thus, we propose an alternative perspective for assessing these public engagement efforts. This view can be constructed through comparing what is taking place in other fields and through illustration of the value of these engagements from the perspective of the ENGOs themselves. Let us use bird watching as an example to demonstrate this point.

According to the State Forestry Administration of China, at the beginning of the millennium, bird watching was still only of interest to a 'few ornithologists' (SFA, 2011). However, as the result of various public education and outreach programmes organised by Beijing environmental groups, there has been a jump in the number of bird-watching societies around the country in the past few years. Currently there are an estimated 50,000 'birders' in China[4] (SFA, 2011). Fu Jianping, director of Beijing's Bird Watching Society, says the transformation of public interest is palpable:

> About ten years ago, when my friend and I first started organising bird-watching events in Beijing, most people had no idea what bird watching was or what it was for. I remember in 2003, whenever we set up the big monocular in the Old Summer Palace in Beijing, tourists would come and ask if we were survey engineers and were there conducting measurements! But it took only three years [to see the ENGO's public outreach initiative bear fruit]. Around 2006 to 2007, whenever we have the monocular set up, there will always be tourists or passers-by coming up for an interesting chat about the birds.

This was echoed by another participant in Beijing, who thought that the popularisation of bird watching has taken on a 'Chinese characteristic':

> Bird watching has a somewhat posh reputation in the West. It's an activity for at least the well-off middle class. But it's quite different in China. Birders in China are from all kinds of social and economic backgrounds. It's rather a hobby of the masses. Its popularity is mostly promoted by various environmental groups, large and small.

It may not be purely an accident that bird watching is a favourite

---

4 See also two major bird-watching websites, <www.cbw.org.cn> and <www.chinabirdnet.org>.

choice among Chinese ENGOs trying to gain public interest in environmental issues. Given that a pair of binoculars is the only equipment required, it is a pastime that has a low technical barrier for mass participation. But more importantly, as Director Fu told us, the population of birds is often a good and sensitive indicator of the local environment. Thus data drawn from the observation of birds provides a convenient and relevant connection to the ecological conditions people live in.

The expansion of China's bird-watching community has provoked collective reflection on social norms and opened up new channels of political involvement in at least three ways. First, it challenges a blind acceptance of development, especially progressive urbanisation. One example is a decade-long campaign to save Beijing's swallow population.

The swallow is a species of bird that especially captures the Chinese imagination. Their annual migration and return are interpreted as representing courage, loyalty, hope and promise, and have inspired many Chinese ancient poems and literature (Chen, 1996). In folklore, swallows are often described as agile and clever. When they come to build their nest under someone's roof, it is considered a sign of impending good fortune or family happiness. Among the four types of swallow living in China, the Beijing swallow, also known as the common swallow (*Apus apus pekinensis*), is perhaps most well known. This is not only because it was chosen as one of the five mascots for China's 2008 Olympics, but also because it has long been a most visible bird, as its main population dwells in the old city centre of Beijing.

Beijing swallows have one peculiar feature. They cannot take off from level ground and thus have to fly from an initial dive. In other words, their flight always starts from a certain height, then they tumble towards the earth in free fall before veering up into the sky. The open girder and beam structures of traditional Chinese houses provide ideal habitats for these swallows.

However, as high rises began to replace traditional houses in Beijing, and increasing number of residents chose to seal their balconies with glass windows to ward off city pollution, the swallows' usual choice of habitat became increasingly limited. Theoretically, there are still a good number of surviving traditional buildings, such as the Old Palace Museum, Beihai Park and other heritage sites, which can accommodate swallows. But almost all of these buildings have had thin wire screens, known as protective nets, installed to keep off birds so as to protect the sites from droppings.

With a dwindling number of potential habitats, the swallow population has suffered a dramatic decrease since the late 1980s (Zhao and Wan, 2012).

It might be thought that Beijing would act almost automatically to save the bird that bears its name, so that Beijingers can once again appreciate the contribution of returning swallows to the lively atmosphere every spring. But many activists told us that the recognition of environment rights and responsibilities cannot be taken for granted. As one environmentalist put it, for a country that has gone through tremendous socio-economic change by progressive development, 'the idea of green can be misconstrued and deceptive': 'Sometimes people think only "controlled nature" can be called "nature", otherwise it is just "wilderness". For example, people think only finely trimmed city gardens or implanted grass can be counted as the results of greening.' Another office clerk in Beijing, an amateur birder, shared a similar view:

If you ask most Beijingers about birds, they might feel puzzled: birds? What birds? Many may think you are talking about sparrows [which were once considered a pest]. Environmental groups have basically reintroduced the strand of China's bird culture [niao wenhua] into society by educating people on how to catch sight of birds around them. This way they learn to see what is happening to their surroundings.

Thus, similar to photography lessons and other forms of public engagement, one of the immediate objectives for local ENGOs in promoting bird watching is to make visible what has been veiled by the drive for a narrowly defined prosperity. Moreover, such events also enable the dwindling swallow population to become a public issue rather than the subject of a mere academic discussion.

This leads to our second point. That is, ENGOs serve as a bridge between the academic community and the public, which itself should be considered as an achievement. Communication between the academic and public spheres in China has been notoriously insufficient. A 2007 national survey on public understanding of science showed a general deficiency of public engagement (Ren, 2008). A separate study also criticised China's 'institutional science communication' as barren, and pointed out that effective public communication of the matter was 'urgently needed'(Jia, 2007). In addition, recent studies on science and biosecurity governance have further suggested a lack of communicative efforts between professional communities and the general public (Barr and Zhang, 2010; J. Y. Zhang, 2012). A key reason for this, as one former popular science editor, Xu Liping, points out, is a lack of communicative infrastructure:

> There is little incentive for individual scientists to initiate a public communicative effort, since traditionally it is the opinion of the technocrats rather than the public that counts in funding and regulatory decisions. For example it is really difficult to persuade them to write a popular science article, because this does not count as one of their professional publications. They question why they should write for an 'unknown mass audience' outside their institutional box.

ENGO events are a medium to break that box and attach human faces to the 'unknown mass audience'. The public events organised by bird-watching societies involve ornithologists, ecologists and relevant urbanisation experts in giving weekend lectures or supervising outdoor observation. Since 2007, the Beijing Bird Watching Society has organised volunteers to work with local scientific researchers in tagging Beijing swallows. That is, they have begun to study the longevity, mortality and territoriality of swallows by banding individually numbered tags to their legs. When we consider the general level of public engagement in China, the routinised public education and events on environment-related issues organised by various ENGOs should in themselves be considered as an achievement.

Third, and related, organised data collection is itself an empowering process for civil participation in policy making. This point will be further demonstrated in Chapter 3. In the case of bird watching, as Director Fu told us,

> We have just taken off, and just harvested initial data sets. It actually took environment groups in Taiwan 10 to 20 years to establish a smooth collaborative relation with their local government. The Chinese government seems to have signalled a certain willingness to collaborate with NGOs. Our next aim would be to take these data to Beijing's municipal government and relevant institutions.

At the time of writing this book, Fu and her colleagues had just publicised their findings based on a five-year programme,

'Investigation and Protection of Swallows and *Apus Apus Pekinensis* in Beijing' (Zhao, 2012; Zhao and Wan, 2012). A couple of weeks prior to the publication of these findings, bird watchers gathered in Tianjin, to attend a 'research sharing' workshop on regional migratory birds (Yi and Liu, 2012). This workshop led to the 'Open Appeal to Establishing Beidagang Wetland National Natural Reserve', which was a collaborative effort involving 110 organisations and 559 volunteers, initiated by academia and coordinated by another Beijing ENGO, the Nature University (Yi and Liu, 2012; Yi, He and Liu, 2012; Nature University, 2012).

In summary, ENGO-organised public outreach and engagement programmes may deserve more credit than they have received in transforming China's civil participation. Underlying the growing popularity of events such as photographic lessons and bird watching is an effective provocation of collective reflection, generating new possibilities for self-empowerment of the grassroots. Our findings are in line with several analyses of China's green activism, which have pointed out that a 'boundary-spanning' framework allows for a better understanding of what is taking place on the ground. This is to say, while avoiding direct confrontation, social actors are taking 'advantage of political grey zones to advance contestable claims and extract concessions' and in the process, are adroitly employing the rhetoric of authority to curb authority itself (Yang, 2005: 52; Ho, 2001).

The Power of Public Gaze

Bird watching and photographic classes may represent what many environmental activists described as 'wielding a discreet influence' (*qianyimohua*), in which the invitation to 'see' nurtures an urge to take action in otherwise indifferent individuals. However, the significance of directing the public's eye to certain social issues is not limited to mass mobilisation. The very act of looking may itself entail an effective response to environmental concerns.

One example is the power of a 'surrounded gaze' (*weiguan*) which forced China Resources Snow Breweries (hereafter Snow Beer) to significantly alter its sponsored brand promotion activity in 2011. As illustrated below, this case concerns first, rival campaigns by two beer producers – in 2008 Snow Beer overtook Bud Light to become the best-selling beer brand in the world (Jones, 2009) – and second, a few grassroots activists. It demonstrates, in recognising the economic and political constraints for direct confrontation, an increasing popular strategy adopted by Chinese environmentalists. This is to build resistance from the bottom up with the help of online and traditional media.

The brand promotion campaign led by Snow Beer was part of its long-term business programme under the slogan 'Brave to the world's end' (*yongchuang tianya*). Since 2005, the company has been working to establish a modern, invigorating and daring brand image. It hosts a nationwide tournament with a different theme each year, in which a small team of consumers are selected to take part in an exploratory adventure, such as a trip to China's Tsangpo Canyon or Taklamakan Desert. In 2011, the theme was 'Traversing beyond Kekexili'.[5] Kekexili, also known as Hoh Xil, is an isolated region in northwestern Tibet. Commonly known as 'no-man's land', Kekexili acts a symbol for Tibet's mysterious natural beauty. To match Kekexili's macho reputation, Snow Beer framed its national campaign as looking for 'warriors' (*yongshi*) who were entitled to enjoy nature's glamour (Guo, 2011). The campaign was launched in summer 2011. In many ways, this campaign fitted perfectly with Snow Beer's brand values, and seemed to be most appealing to young consumers. The title itself suggested a celebration of courageousness, an admiration of those who continually challenge constraints, and an ambition to exceed their limits.

However, Kekexili is an NNR. According to the degree of accessibility stated by the 18th clause of the Nature Reserve Regulation of the People's Republic of China (State Council, 1994), any NNR consists of three areas:

- The inner core protection area which bans all entry of all parties. In other words, it is an intended no-man's land.
- The middling cushion area which allows authorized entry for protective and research purposes.
- The outer experimental area to which the local bureau has the discretion of granting selective entry for research, teaching and tourism.

In addition, Kekexili has a special place in the history of China's environmental protection measures. Despite being home to 230 types of wildlife and having been exposed to illegal gold mining, it was not entitled to the protection of NNR status until 1995, when a local vigilante ranger was shot dead by bands of chiru poachers.

---

5 See <www.yongchuang.snowbeer.com.cn>.

This story later inspired the award-winning 2004 film *Kekexili: Mountain Patrol*, which made Kekexili a household name. For many environmentalists we interviewed, 'defending Kekexili', a campaign that took place after the shocking incident, was a milestone in China's green movement, as it promoted the profile of ecological preservation in less developed parts of China.

Thus when Wang Zhen, a self-employed businessman, watched Snow Beer's campaign on television, he felt very uncomfortable. Wang Zhen had once been an environmental volunteer working on the protection of Kekexili. At the time he learned of Snow Beer's plan, Wang had, in his words, 'drifted away' from an environmental focus and had devoted himself to wider civil society initiatives along the east coast of China. His reason was that after being involved with various preservation campaigns in the Qinghai-Tibetan Plateau, he had come to the conclusion that China's environmental problems could only be better addressed by a stronger civil society. Thus he 'retired' to Wenzhou, a southern manufacturing town, and campaigned on local issues. He felt immediate concern about Snow Beer's widely publicised brand campaign, however. On the one hand, travel across the heart of Kekexili, which the advertising implied was the intention of the venture, would be illegal. On the other hand, if the actual plan was only to visit the peripheral regions of Kekexili, not only was the advertisement misleading, it sent out the wrong message about the region. As Wang explained, 'An NNR is meant to be protected and preserved, not to be conquered or traversed.' Thus, Wang decided to demand that Snow Beer publicise the precise travel arrangements it had agreed with the local protection bureau at Kekexili.

Before we got in touch with Wang, we had got the impression from following news sources and online discussions that a confrontation was developing fast, with both sides keeping a close watch on the other's moves. Wang claimed on Weibo that he had phoned the Kekexili nature reserve office, and gained the impression that Snow Beer had paid a healthy sum of money to enable its team to enter the core area. A couple of Beijing ENGOs, most notably Green Beagle, helped to publicise Wang's concerns. This stirred the attention of Chinese netizens who were watchful for potential corruption. A workshop was held in Beijing, with participants representing the ENGOs and Snow Beer, with the initial aim of reconciling the dispute. However, no resolution was reached (Green Beagle, 2011; Yi, 2011). Snow Beer refused to disclose its travel arrangement in full, and the environmentalists were obviously not prepared to relent. Snow Beer then adopted the tactic of advertising the company's past contribution to environmental protection (China News, 2011). However, at the same time environmental volunteers found that a number of Snow Beer factories were suspected of illegal waste dumping. Photos of the factory waste were posted online as evidence. As a result of this move, the ENGO campaign against Snow Beer started to win more supporters. The company's travel plan was leaked to Wang, apparently by disgruntled employees, followed by versions of the company's revised Kekexili programme plans in response to the new evidence that had been put online. Although it never made headline news, in the months that followed there was a fair amount of media coverage of the dispute (Li, 2011; Yi, 2011).

One week before the scheduled departure of Snow Beer's exploration party in late 2011, one of the authors, Zhang, got in touch with Wang Zhen through a friend. At the time, Wang and his colleagues knew through insider information that Snow Beer had significantly changed its travel plan. But in the eyes of the environmentalists, even the latest revised travel plan was far from being ecologically friendly. Both sides were said to have prepared backup plans: one to ensure commercial publicity success, the other to minimize environmental impact. Needless to say, it was a sensitive time.

As soon as she had introduced herself, Wang anxiously asked Zhang, 'Are you a journalist?' In fairness this was not an uncommon question during our fieldwork. As environmental activism remained politically sensitive, many activists were cautious of how their efforts were framed, because any media misrepresentation could potentially undermine their efforts. Zhang immediately assured him that this was part of a research project, and neither he and nor his friends would find reports of anything he said the next day in either the English or Chinese popular media. In fact, we assured him that given the time it usually takes to publish academic papers, his project would have long concluded before our research findings were published.

We assumed this was what Wang wanted to hear, but we were wrong. Wang slowly responded, 'I am not concerned that you will bring me trouble. But I am anxious to make more people aware of what we are doing here and help us to stop Snow Beer together.'

We soon understood Wang's interest in getting more media attention. With his experience in environmental protection, he was fully aware of the constraints on grassroots organizations. He had far less political influence than Snow Beer. He did not have institutional support or connections, nor did he have the financial influence to force the media to pull unfavourable reports, as Snow Beer had done. Despite the fact that many ENGOs felt sympathetic to his cause, few had financial resources or labour to spare because they were all committed to their own ongoing projects Wang's campaign had started with only a computer and an internet connection before his brother and his friend Zhou Xiang were persuaded to join him.

Even this three-man team had taken Wang some effort to organize, for they all had a realistic view of the constraints on grassroots campaigns, and had questioned what they could actually achieve by publicly confronting a business giant. For example, Zhou Xiang confessed that he went through cycles of pessimism. He had heard of Snow Beer's exploration plan long before Wang had contacted him. Zhou was sure that in the absence of institutional support, this tiny campaign group would not be able to 'achieve anything', so he had not planned to take any action until Wang persuaded him to take on the challenge. As he put it, 'I agreed to help because I agree [with Wang] that if the government fails to implement its legislation, then it depends on us at the grassroots to stand up and speak out for the public .... If we find a company organises an irresponsible public event, then we should let others know why it is wrong.'

Like most activists, Wang and his friends started with Weibo and blogging, and asked all their acquaintances to re-tweet their updates on the event. The messages slowly spread out into the public domain. Through friends of friends, Wang was interviewed by a few traditional media and a couple of key portal sites, such as Netease and Sina.

'I know we cannot do much. But we can rely on the power of the public gaze (*weiguan*).' This was how Wang saw the campaign strategy, 'Public gaze is a way of protesting as well as a form of dissuasion.' He was referring here to the phrase 'uninformed public gazing in a circle' (*buming zhenxiang qunzhong weiguan*), a popular expression among Chinese netizens to express scepticism about events and to demand transparency of information. He told us:

My aim is to circle them [Snow Beer] with public scrutiny. Let them know they are being watched: We are watching their every move on this issue and through us, countless members of the general public are also watching how they respond. Although we have no authority to take any action and have little influence on Snow Beer, the fact that someone knows they are being watched is enough to have some impact.

For Wang, the accumulated gazes themselves form a force for change. Although by the time we met there were a few media reports on this issue, it was a hard-won attention. Zhou recounted that when he asked others to join the appeal, some were touched, some were indifferent, and many considered it, as Zhou himself had once believed, a futile attempt.

The Kekexili NNR office largely remained silent in the months of argument. Wang said that to some extent he sympathised with the officials, because allowing in a few jeeps for a quick run through the reserve would bring in a meaningful amount of income. But there was a danger that it could create a slippery slope for future companies wanting to organise similar events.

In the end, Wang and Zhou's campaign was not completely futile. Although Snow Beer did not cancel the Kekexili trip, it eventually chose a relatively undamaging route near the edge of the nature reserve. Given the scarce social resources Wang had at his disposal, this was a moderate but still impressive success. Zhou did not find the final outcome 'particularly satisfying' as in his view, the four months of work only suggested that much more needed to be done to enhance public understanding of environmental protection.

Wang and his friends later (re)established the Kekexili Volunteer Communication Centre based on existing networks of individuals concerned about Kekexili preservation. Wang intentionally kept this centre independent of the official volunteer programme run by the Kekexili NNR. He preferred to call the group the 'Kekexili V Team'. The letter V is obviously an abbreviation for 'volunteer', but it is perhaps also a reference to the Alan Moore story *V for Vendetta*, in which the masked revolutionary 'V' battled against a totalitarian government. The image of 'V' became a popular icon for civil movements in China in 2009, as it was used in a widespread Anonymous Netizen (*Niming Wangmin Xuanyan*) campaign to protest against the Chinese government's heightened censorship. In this sense, the letter V is also a demonstration of dissent against Kekexili NNR's perceived irresponsibility.

It is difficult to evaluate the impact of the discussion on Snow Beer's trip to Kekexili in 2011. Wang and his friends brought about little institutional change in the operation of the NNR. Yet the very fact that a small-town businessman with a computer had built up a public gaze that pressured a domestic industrial giant to think twice about its commercial activity was itself a triumph. The impact of Wang's initiative may have been limited to this one-off event, but its social significance can perhaps only be understood when taking into account the bigger picture.

Wang viewed his V Team as similar to many of China's civil efforts. He made the analogy that grassroots initiatives were like eggs attempting to strike a stone wall, an endeavour that was doomed to failure, but nonetheless valuable:

> Even within the current political system, sometimes it seems we change nothing, but what we [environmental groups] do is still worthwhile. Because I see our job as hitting the walls, the barriers that confine us. Many people have leapt over the walls, but for those who are still inside, we need to constantly strike against the wall. Of course if you hit a stone wall with an egg, it will always be the egg that gets hurt. The case of Kekexili is an example, the government office and commercial company all have so much capital at hand. They stood as walls that we must strike against. I'm not too worried about the final outcome: maybe the walls remain untouched, but maybe they will become dented. But we must keep on striking against them. That's to say we must monitor how things operate in our society. Of course, we cannot just blindly hit the wall. You need to be sensible and strategic.

Wang's comments suggest a balance between pessimistic realism and the audacity of hope. To paraphrase environmentalist Tang Xiyang's interpretation of the green movement cited in the Introduction, Wang and his friend engaged with the campaign, not so much because they were striving for immediate empowerment and victory, but in defiance of constraints and despair.

Ways of Seeing and Ways of Weighing

There are different ways of perceiving the value of grassroots green activism in China. Different measurements can be used in weighing its significance. A conventional approach is to juxtapose bottom-up initiatives with consequential institutional change or the level of policy influence. Viewed from this perspective, China's domestic ENGOs still have a long way to go, as more than half of the organisations mentioned in this chapter are not fully registered as NGOs with local authorities. However, when examined on a case to case basis we can see moderate success in the changes green activists aim to bring into society. Underground NGOs are fully operational 'overground' (as in the case of photographic lessons);

they collect scientific data and make policy appeals (as in the case of bird protection), and they dare to challenge commercial giants (as in the case of Kekexili). It does not make sense that the passion and efforts amount to nothing 'significant', while at the same time the events they organise are clearly winning popularity and are becoming an integral part of society. The seeming contradiction of the non-(policy)-impact and emerging social force begs the question: where did the social 'significance' go? It is not the absence of government approval that incapacitates grassroots actions. But it may be an institutional-centric framework that prematurely invalidates bottom-up contributions and fails to see their significance.

We must, of course, also be cautious of not overestimating the influence of grassroots activism. After all even activists themselves know they 'cannot do much' (Wang Zhen) and do not take any achievement for granted. Song Ming, co-founder of an underground ENGO which aims to bring together academics and the general public, shared a similar view. She described the growth and value of her organisation as a constant struggle between an acknowledged political uncertainty and a solid determination:

> Honestly, sometime we are also in doubt why we sacrifice our free time doing it. What keeps us in action is the mere fact that we can do something [about the environment], and some action is better than none. I guess many people share this view or else we won't have an expanding number of members .... Grand ideas and visions are great but we need to develop a linkage between these ambitions with ordinary Chinese and everyday trivial issues .... In terms of how big our organisation can grow, how long it will survive, I have no idea, nor do I worry too much. We take one step at a time.

The green movement in China may well be described as an entanglement of despair and hope. While it is important to locate the institutional source of despair (in an authoritarian government), it is just as important to understand the origin of hope.

This chapter aimed to address this question by first examining what environmental issues are worth fighting for in the eyes of grassroots activists. This is crucial to comprehend how they evaluate what needs to be done and how they identify their role in the greening of China. In the three cases demonstrated in this chapter, the focus was on evoking public reflection on society's norms, such as progressive urbanisation, the disappearing ecological base for culture, and the daring spirit in subduing nature.

It is worth noting that educational activities are not limited to underground NGOs. In fact, the importance of continuous public engagement was highlighted by many leading environmentalists in China. One example is Liao Xiaoyi, founder of the preeminent ENGO Global Village Beijing, who has decided to return to public education in recent years. The reason was that after more than a decade working on environmental protection, Liao found China's degrading environment could only be saved through increased public consciousness. She wrote in 2008 '[when] a mountain no longer looks like a [green] mountain, when the water no longer exhibits the purity of water, that's because the people are losing their humanity' (Liao, 2008).

As in the quote from Tang Peng cited earlier, a priority for Chinese ENGOs are to wake up 'resources and social energies that are in deep sleep in China'. In this sense, the social implications of environmental initiatives in China bear resemblance to the situation in Eastern Europe in the 1980s. That is, they are not just about the environment, but evoke a more general reflection on the humanness of modern life and the consciousness of environment rights and responsibilities.

Chinese green activists share a faith in an informed society. Most of these public engagement events do not provide a structured education programme but have the aim to inform people, through dissemination of scientific facts, co-production of ecological statistics, or increasing transparency. We argue that the proliferation of public engagement events by ENGOs in China is a big deal. For a society that has developed with its government monopolising information, to inform is to empower. How an empowered group of public take action is the focus of the next chapter.

3 WAYS OF CHANGING

As with many researchers in Europe, our research on Chinese green politics actually started in the West. Our first knowledge of China's grassroots activism came from journal articles and conferences framed in familiar academic discourses. Before we set off to do our fieldwork, our initial contacts were established through our colleagues, such as staff at international ENGOs and visiting scholars at British and French universities.

It would be no exaggeration to say that although there have been a few high-profile cases of ENGO influence, such as the public consultations over the Dujiangyan dam and the Nujiang hydropower station, many people hold the view that Chinese domestic ENGOs in general lack the ability to establish an enduring influence or prompt meaningful institutional reform (Knup, 1997; Ma, 2005; Lu, 2007). As one professor from Renmin University put it, 'none of the rights-defending initiatives [in China] last long. They are often one-off events.' Another former World Wide Fund for Nature (WWF) staff member described her general impression of home-grown ENGOs as 'they are full of passion, but that seems to be all they have'. Chinese literature on this topic often echoes a similar view. Civil environmental groups have been criticised for being devoid of 'the capability of conducting empirical studies and setting up professional dialogues, and [they also] lack the ability to avail [themselves of] legal channels in seeking effective [environmental] protections' (Feng, 2009: 185).

In short, Chinese green activism is often described as 'intra-system operations' (*tizhinei caozuo*) (Hong, 2007). This phrase signifies that given Beijing's intolerance to opposition, societal campaigns must operate within existing political frameworks and institutions. While this observation has truth to it, the more we get to know grassroots ENGOs in China, the more we feel it may convey a false impression of Chinese activists as being passive and submissive. It is somewhat misguided to dismiss the impact of green activism in China on the basis of government intolerance and restrictions. In fact, from the perspective of Chinese grassroots, even within the system there is still much that is worth doing (for example rights to be secured, rules to be established, opinions to be voiced). More relevant questions are what are the channels and norms in handling disputes, and how are these options being shaped? One example is Su Rui, who is in her late 20s and has volunteered for both an American and a southern Chinese ENGO since her university days. After graduation, she chose to work for a domestic NGO, as she felt international ENGOs had little idea of what should be done in China. We met during her campaign for financial compensation for a small southern village for pollution damage. We questioned why she sought immediate financial payment rather than taking the case to court to demand a change in the law. She gave a light laugh and told us:

> You are too academic to solve Chinese problems. We don't define the needs of the people we help. Sometimes we go for lawsuits, sometimes we don't. We ask what the villagers want and we act on their needs. For them [the specific case she was working on at the time], it's too arduous to wait for legal solutions. They need cash for their medications and their basic subsistence.

Another activist who worked in a domestic ENGO in Beijing also puzzled us when she said she valued transnational dialogue but was not keen on collaborating with Western NGOs. She explained that this is because of the different value systems at work:

> For example, when we investigated local illegal dumping in inner western China, all they [Western collaborators] cared about was to come up with policy recommendations, and they chase up on you to find a channel to pass this on. So that they can establish the record that they have the paperwork read by the some officials. This may have been useful in their country, but how will that help the victims or solve the problem here in China?

This is not to say that domestic ENGOs are indifferent or opposed to having a regulatory impact. As explained by Su, sometimes they 'go for lawsuits and sometimes [they] don't'. The difference relies on the fact that they 'don't define the needs of the people [they] help'. To be sure, this is to some extent shaped by China's political culture. But it could also be argued that it is because of a different sense of immediacy and a different (and perhaps more adapted) awareness of what needs to be done. It seems that grassroots ENGOs have quite different understandings of what can be considered as 'impact', or to put it more bluntly, 'usefulness'. Rather than approaching environmental concerns systematically with categorical aims, such as making policy, economic or ethical statements, they exhibit a strong pragmatic problem-solving orientation.

This chapter continues to investigate the social habitus of green activism. It focuses especially on how this pragmatic orientation contributes to the social milieu in which ENGOs are situated in. We take two recent examples of China's green activism: one is a nation-wide air-quality campaign, the other is local pollution caused by Apple's Chinese suppliers. In each of the cases analysed below, we want to highlight three points:

- how the case study was perceived in the eyes of the Chinese
- ENGOs' framing of state–society relations and the building of legitimacy through the sharing of information
- strategies of synthesising social resources and the instrumentalisation of existing rules and norms.

We argue that grassroots environmental actors can be a greater force for change than they are often given credit for being.

Clean Air with Chinese Characteristics

In classic economics, a free good, or common good, is a key concept used to describe a certain resource that is in great abundance and whose supply incurs zero opportunity cost to the society. Textbook examples are sunshine, water and fresh air.

As of September 17, 2012, however, with the marketing of 'Chen Guangbiao canned fresh air' in Beijing, Shanghai and Guangzhou, these classic examples have been subject to revision. The brand name refers to the man behind this new enterprise. Chen Guangbiao, who prefers to be called 'Low-Carbon Chen', is head of a resource recycling company in Jiangsu, on the southeast coast of China.

Chen's canned air can looks similar to a soft drink can, but it contains Grade 2 quality air bottled by hand from a dozen remote locations, such as minority regions in the southwestern part of China and underdeveloped areas which once served as revolutionary bases for Mao Zedong (Peng, 2012). Each can is marketed at 4 to 5 RMB (40–50p), almost equivalent to two and a half cans of Coca-Cola in Beijing. Even though Chen's cans contain a computer chip to preserve and compress the fresh air (CNR, 2012), their consumption is fairly intuitive. During the press conference at one of Beijing's most luxurious venues, the Shangri-la Hotel, Chen demonstrated the three steps involved in enjoying the product: first you open the can, then you put your nose near the top of the can, and finally you breathe in.

It must be mentioned that Chen is perhaps better known as 'China's Number One Philanthropist' (*zhongguo shoushan*) and has reportedly donated approximately 1.5 billion RMB (£150 million) to charitable causes since 1998. He is also known for his controversial love of publicity (Wei, 2010). Thus, at the launch of his latest product, there was a moment of confusion among Chinese news commentators on whether this should be presented as 'a green initiative' or as 'performance art' (F. Y. Zhang, 2012).

The irony of this news seemed obvious enough. This was perhaps a market with 'Chinese characteristics'. With degrading air quality in an increasing number of cities, oxygen itself seemed to have become a profitable scarcity and simple biological intuitions (that is, the act of breathing) turned into detailed instructions on how to consume.

But Chen wasn't just making a public statement. For him, this meant real business with a promising market. At the product launch, the revenue was already projected to top 100 million RMB in the coming year (CNR, 2012). In fact, apart from the canned product, Chen was also planning to set up a network of retail stores in residential areas. Compressed fresh air would be transported in barrels to local stores, providing 'refill' options to reduce the waste of cans. Alternatively, home delivery services could be provided. As Chen explained, 'it is just like your milk delivery' (CNR, 2012).

For some analysts, the idea of marketing air was not as radical as it sounded. One commentary in *Guangzhou Daily* noted that such thoughts can be linked back to global climate action:

The rectification of the Kyoto Protocol in 2005 has set a binding framework on developed countries' greenhouse gas emissions. Carbon trade was thus born out of the combination of high reduction cost and technical difficulties common in developed countries and the comparatively lower cost and existing reduction possibilities in the developing countries. This is not only a market approach in solving the problem with greenhouse gas emission reduction, but accredited air with marketable value .... In this sense, carbon trade and Chen's air vending use the same principle.

(F. Y. Zhang, 2012)

The mass marketing of fresh air was shocking nonetheless. Not so much in its conceptual novelty, but in the empirical implication that the perceived scarcity of fresh air was significant enough to generate revenue! It seemed to imply that at least for white-collar workers in major Chinese cities, the source of clean air was so distant from their life that it had to be treated like milk, which needs to be collected, sterilised, purchased and most importantly 'supplied on demand' through commercial companies.

The Politicisation of PM2.5

During the 1980s, China's particulate matter (PM) air pollution level was 10–16 times higher than the World Health Organization's (WHO's) annual guidelines (Matus et al., 2012: 64). Terms such as 'acid rain' and 'atmospheric suspended matter' were already being reported by the media and attracted moderate political attention by municipal governments in major cities like Beijing and Guangzhou at the end of 1990s (Xiao and Xu, 2008; PUESC, 1999). A recent study estimated that the socio-economic burden created by air pollution alone may have cost up to US$112 billion loss of welfare and US$69 billion loss in consumption in China's economy (Matus et al., 2012: 61–2). But public concern over air quality is relatively a recent thing. Looking back, canned fresh air was perhaps already needed in Beijing during the days of the '*Titanic* effect' rain mentioned at the beginning of Chapter 2. But such a market was not recognised until recently.

As with many other basic public services in China, for the larger part of the last few decades, air quality control was considered a task for the government. More importantly, with the centralisation of resources and top-down administrative culture, the government seemed to be the only agent that had any real capacity to act on collective affairs. This point is important, since as further discussed in this section, the national air quality campaign that was initiated in 2011 indicated a significant shift of mentality regarding state dominance of this issue.

To be sure, most of the early efforts were government-led. For example, in 1998 Beijing raised the standards for coal and fuel, and reinforced the mandatory dust control of construction sites (Xiao and Xu, 2008; PUESC, 1999). Many provincial authorities followed suit. From 1997 onwards, Guangzhou gradually tightened its regulation of automobile exhaust gas pollution (PUESC, 1999).

A more recent example of government-led air control was the 2008 Beijing Olympic Games. Given bad publicity over its air quality, the government sought to close the gap between Beijing's environmental profile and its supposed cosmopolitan stature (Aldhous, 2005; Madrigal, 2008). It did this through the relocation or forced temporary closure of factories, piping in natural gas, and operating a scheme of alternate driving days for traffic restriction. Similar measures were taken in other major cities where Olympic events were held. To be sure, it created much inconvenience. The phrase '*bi-yun*' became a popular phonetic sarcasm as it represents both 'contraception' and 'to avoid the Olympics'. But these temporary measures also delivered obvious environmental effects. Beijing's sky started to clear. If it was a shock to Beijingers to see how much their lifestyle had to change in order to achieve a 'normal' sky, then it was with a mixture of bewildered indignation and humiliation that they saw footage of American athletes arriving in the capital wearing masks. There were different interpretations of the arrival of Olympians arriving with protection against Beijing's skies. Some saw it as an arrogant display of Western discrimination against China, while some saw it as a worrying sign that even the improved air was considered by foreigners as too risky to breathe (Macur, 2008; He, 2008).

At the time most Chinese remained hopeful, as the Beijing government promised continuous efforts in improving air quality. In addition, a United Nations Environment Programme assessment carried out from 2007 to December 2008 also confirmed that 'that Beijing raised the environmental bar and the Games left a lasting legacy for the city' (UNEP, 2009). However the level of commitment didn't seem to last and Beijing was soon trapped in pollution again (Spencer, 2008). Similar cycles of temporary pollution reduction and forgotten pledges happened for the World Expo in Shanghai and the Asian Games in Guangzhou in 2010. After the three international events, it was business as usual again, with all three cities soon plagued by smog (Master, 2010).

The seemingly empty promises were not simply a dereliction of duty by municipal governments, as Zhu Can, program officer at the Clean Air Initiative for Asian Cities (CAI-Asia), told us. They reflected a more embedded structural problem with China's political conventions:

The Beijing Olympics, Shanghai Expo and Guangzhou Asian Games all provided valuable experience to local pollution control. All relevant data were obliged to be shared among different administrative branches. But these initiatives delivered the data because they were subject to powerful top-down political command and government pressures. These collaborative channels were put aside after these major events. Every office started to take care of its own business. For example, if Shanghai, Suzhou and Zhejiang [neighbouring administrative authorities] can collaborate in locating their industries, the environmental impact will be much reduced. ... [The reason is that] air quality is not a matter that can be confined to a specific city, but requires regional governance. For example, small particulates such as PM2.5 can flow in the air and travel for a long distance. Pollutants in Beijing's air may not be generated in Beijing, but may come from Hebei.

Thus the problem is not merely whether or not a particular local authority wants to improve air quality. As we discuss in Chapter 5, under China's fragmented governance structure, there is little incentive for coordinated actions or data sharing. The PM2.5 Zhu mentions is a term for particulate matter less than 2.5 micrometres in diameter, which is believed to pose serious health risks. Most developed countries in North America and Europe and a number of Asian countries, such as Japan, India and Thailand, have adopted PM2.5 levels as an indicator for national environmental monitoring. Yet as of the writing of this book in summer 2012, PM2.5 monitoring in China was used mainly in research and was not employed as a standard for measuring air quality. Nor were China's PM2.5 levels considered to be public information. The time frame for the national inclusion of a PM2.5 standard was set as 2016, although Beijing was set to employ PM2.5 measurement in 2013 (Jin, 2012b; Pan, 2012).

PM2.5 might have remained professional jargon in China if it had not been for the independent monitoring and hourly publication of air quality data conducted by the US Embassy in Beijing since the spring of 2008 (Bradsher, 2012; Wu, 2011). Reportage of the US Embassy's air monitoring appeared in 2009, but it was dismissed by Chinese environment experts on different occasions as 'not scientific', since they claimed spot data cannot be generalised to represent the whole city's air quality (Zhao, 2009; Wu, 2011). This is a point recognised by the US Embassy in Beijing, as it stated on its online disclaimer that 'citywide analysis cannot be done, however, on data from a single machine'.[1] But as the smog has persisted in many

---

1 <www.beijing.usembassy-china.org.cn>.

Chinese cities, an increasing number of Chinese have accessed the US Embassy data on Weibo and smartphone apps. There are plenty of examples when the US data indicated a pollution level that could be described as 'crazy bad' or 'beyond index' but the Chinese official data suggested only 'minor pollution' (Ramzy, 2012).

Since 2010, PM2.5 levels have gradually become a big issue in China's pubic domain, especially after the government's perceived inadequate action. According to *Time* magazine, 'China first complained privately about the U.S. embassy's air-quality monitoring in 2009, telling U.S. diplomats in a heated meeting that it might cause confusion amongst the Chinese public and lead to "social consequences"' (Ramzy, 2012). When the MEP revised its 'Environment Air Quality Standards' (*huanjing kongqi zhiliang biaozhun*) in 2010, PM2.5 was not included as a pollutant for which monitoring was required as many expected, but only listed as a local referencing pollutant (Feng and Lv, 2011). The reason given was that that adopting PM2.5 standards was still premature for 'Chinese particularities' (*zhongguo guoqing*) (Xun, 2011).

'Chinese particularities' might be regarded as an elixir by the government in its attempt to mend its relations with society. It underlies a developing country mentality which suggests any injustice is transitory and justifiable. However, it seems to be a weak excuse in the eyes of most Chinese. Major cities such as Beijing were known to have the capacity to monitor PM2.5, but were seen to be reluctant to release the data. There are a number of reasons for the government's resistance to adopting PM2.5 as a reference measure. But one chief consideration, as China's most vocal newspaper, *Southern Weekend*, pointed out, was the unpredictable political implications: 'if PM2.5 is not included in the air quality evaluation index, then more than 70% of Chinese cities can be said to have "quality air"'; but if China's national quality control measures incorporate the WHO's PM2.5 standards, then 'the qualifying rate may drop to 20%' (Feng and Lv, 2011).

In short, PM2.5 levels have long been a subject of academic study. But publicising them became a political problem, not just because of the availability of comparable data generated by the US Embassy, but also because of the perceived incompetence of Chinese local authorities and the forgotten political promises after their hosting of international events.

As poor-quality air cannot be justified by the usual excuse of 'Chinese particularities', a nation-wide grassroots movement initiated an air monitoring and data-sharing system, known as 'I

Monitor the Air for My Country'. In contrast to the government pushing an agenda onto society, this public campaign applied pressure from the bottom up in pressing for better air quality controls. Zhong Nanshan, a nationally respected respiratory disease expert, termed this a 'reverse coercion' (*dao bi*) of political actions (J. Wang, 2012).

'I Monitor the Air for My Country'

At the beginning of 2011, the Beijing ENGO Green Beagle was conducting a study on indoor pollution caused by cigarette smoking. Its primary data collection consisted of using compact PM2.5 monitors to read indoor air quality in public buildings. As the US Embassy's single-spot reading was criticised by the government as biased (Zhao, 2009; Wu, 2011), Green Beagle staff soon had the idea that if these monitors were handed out to ordinary people who agreed to carry them around, it would establish a PM2.5 trail for the individual. If users kept records of their movements (time and location), such an exercise could help to create an aggregate record of Beijing's air quality at diverse locations at different times of the day. The data set would be still too random for it to be possible to make reliable scientific deductions from it, but it would make a much stronger social statement on air quality. In addition, as Fan Xiaqiu, the person in charge of organising the event told us, it would be a great way to engage with the general public.

This idea received support from China's main portal website, Sina. In its environment protection online channel, Sina set up a webpage for the event, 'My Air Quality Diary: Monitoring the Air around Us Together', mainly directed by Green Beagle.[2] In the summer of 2011, two dozen volunteers carried the compact monitors wherever they went for a whole month. All data was published through the internet. Together they provided a pretty comprehensive, though still rough, civic map of air quality in Beijing.

This was the beginning of what became a nation-wide 'I Monitor the Air for My Country' movement. Not long after the Green Beagle experiment, the idea of inviting public participation in PM2.5 monitoring was soon picked up by a number of environment groups in different Chinese cities. The name of the movement was taken from the title of a report 'I Monitor the Air for My Country' which appeared in *Southern Weekend* in late 2011 (Feng and Lv, 2011). Local monitoring initiatives then adapted generic names, such as

---

2 See <http://event.weibo.com/165698>.

'I Monitor the Air for (my) Tianjin', 'I Monitor the Air for (my) Wuhan', ' I Monitor the Air for (my) Shanghai' and so on.

This *Southern Weekend* article gave great publicity to the campaign. The piece was published along with a cartoon, imitating China's old propaganda posters. Two young men and one young woman occupied the lower right section of the cartoon, looking ahead with a firm and hopeful gaze. The woman was in front and dressed as an engineer ready for action, while a blueprint unfolded before her. The two men were both in plain shirts with sleeves rolled up, posing in classic revolutionary postures. They had one arm raised high and the other holding not a gun or grenade, but a detector and pollutant reader. Lines of red flags flew behind them and a modern high-rise skyline ran across the lower third of the carton. On the upper right-hand corner was a caption, 'As the government continuously put the inclusion of PM2.5 as air quality indicators on hold, civil monitoring initiatives sprouted like bamboo shoots after the spring rain, forming a coercing pressure for the government to take action' (Feng and Lv, 2011). The article further described monitoring efforts as 'grassroots self-redemption, with a kind of firm determination that is made almost without choice (*wunai*)' (Feng and Lv, 2011).

The popularity that the title of the article, 'I Monitor the Air for My Country', quickly gained among ENGOs in China was perhaps because it accurately captured a sense of 'self-redemptive patriotism' which embodied two conflicting sentiments shared by the grassroots.

First, these monitoring projects took advantage of an existing nationalist rhetoric in justifying and legitimising their actions both to the authorities and to the public. It is important to note that these projects were presented as action 'for my country' (rather than 'against' it). This was not only a simple strategy to win public sympathy, and appease local authorities, but also reflected a more pragmatic political value that many Chinese environmental activists want to promote. That is, almost all the green activists we interviewed said that these monitoring schemes were essentially aimed at improving air quality. Monitoring was not an excuse for antagonistic political provocation, but was considered as an effective (and in the eyes of a few, the only) way to pressure the government for an acceleration of environmental progress within China. Fan Qiuxia, the key promoter of this movement, saw the role of ENGOs as facilitators rather than replacements for government programmes:

Our goal is not to establish a rival civic authority on air quality to the government data set. It is impossible to yield scientifically comprehensive and reliable data from the compact machines we are using .... We just want to use this volunteering process as a way to get more people involved, and get people into the discussion of how it is related to our lives. The sooner it [PM2.5] becomes a topic everybody is talking about on the street, the sooner the government will feel the pressure to publicise its data and adapt a monitoring system.

It could be said that domestic ENGOs know their limits, as Fan implies, as they do not have the necessary social resources or stature to directly pressure or negotiate with the government. But they also know their strength. They can turn and steer the public to demand social change.

Chen Qi, campaigning for PM2.5 monitoring in Shenzhen, expressed a similar objective. For him, air monitoring was not about a challenge to political dominance, but a struggle for the right to know and a better enforcement of the law:

Grassroots air monitoring for the country or respective cities is good, but it cannot be the goal or the norm. Within the Chinese political infrastructure, professional and consistent environmental supervision ultimately relies on government commitment. But we [civil actors] can advance that process and make it happen sooner, be implemented better. For example, I've been campaigning for PM2.5 monitoring since 2010. Shenzhen city council did release its data to the public, but there were days where there was no record, or explanation for the absence of record. There are also cases where among the six districts supposed to be monitored, only one district's data was shown and the rest was missing. As we cannot verify the conclusion ourselves, how can the government expect the citizens to believe in the official air rating? So the grassroots should voice their concerns, let their demands be heard. But the masses have to admit their limits too and not be blind from seeing others' strength. Long-term monitoring should be institutionalised with the professionals.

To some extent, this campaign is not a negation of government efforts and a demand for an alternative, but rather a protest about the sloppiness of institutional work. It is as much a campaign for better air quality as for a 'professionalisation' of government bureaucracies.

Interestingly, in the eyes of grassroots ENGOs, this non-confrontational principle was not a weakness, but added to their maturity and trustworthiness in the eyes of the Chinese public. For example, PM2.5 was not the first civil monitoring programme that Fan Xiaqiu had run. In fact, she and her colleagues at Green Beagle had run free public services for several years to test electromagnetic pollution, indoor formaldehyde pollution, noise pollution and water quality.[3] Anyone living within the greater Beijing area can submit a simple application stating where and which type of pollutant they want to be tested, and have a monitoring visit arranged. These free tests were mostly done with portable equipment on loan from research institutions, and with a professional explaining the data to the individuals who had requested the test. According to Fan, because of a general rise in anxiety about the urban environment and a general deficiency in scientific knowledge, many of the requests they received turned out not to be because there were actual environment hazards, but because of people's misconceptions. Thus, a large part of the work involved disseminating information to provide reassurances about people's safety. For example, Fan received a number of requests to test electromagnetic pollution levels in Beijing. 'In fact, there were only few cases where the electromagnetic strength was harmful to health,' she explained, 'but most people didn't even have an inkling about what electromagnetic radiation was and what generates it. So they were worried and suspected everything. We were there to help people, not to stir up unfounded anxieties.' In cases when Fan and her colleagues found a high level of pollutants that bore health risks, they were not hesitant in advising the community to take the issue to court.

When we explored Green Beagle's website, we found that while the organisation publicises all its test results, it also puts up a disclaimer stating that the data, although collected by trained personnel, should not be used as evidence in court. We wondered if such voluntary self-disaccreditation would send out a wrong image to the public. Fan said it was quite the opposite: 'We are the watchdogs on pollution, but we also want to be a constructive and professional force in promoting the rule of law and help society get use to these ideas.'

To some extent, such rationales could be interpreted as working

---

3 See <www.bjep.org.cn/pages/detect/detectcenterintro.jsp>.

within and beyond Chinese political particularities. This work was done within the infrastructure, as the initiatives were aimed at neither replacing existing authorities nor imposing drastic restructuring. Rather, they were designed to pressure, accelerate and influence what the Chinese government has acknowledged as possible channels for improvement. At the same time, the initiatives operated beyond the existing infrastructure, as they were also aimed at reinforcing the application of basic political principles (such as the rule of law) to both the authorities and the public.

Thus, the green movement in China has a political agenda. Its agenda is to reinforce the contract between state and society, and to question, assess, and shape those relations. As was pointed out earlier, the issue of air quality was only recently problematised in the public domain. The exposure to an international gaze and Chinese authorities' subsequent failure in fulfilling their environment promises caused social criticism. In this context, being the 'watchdog' and redirecting complaints to existing channels is an exercise of rights, but for contemporary Chinese society, it is perhaps also a necessary reminder of government obligations.

In summary, the first perspective of the two intertwining sentiments captured by the movement 'I Monitor the Air for My Country' was a sense of keeping watch on and aiding the socio-political system. However, being non-confrontational does not mean that there was no contention, which leads to our second point. In the air monitoring project, 'a loss of public trust' (Tong, 2012) towards the authorities also led to a general reflection on state–society relations. There were two main areas of contention. One was the state's obligation to provide transparency, the other was society's rights to supervise the state.

When we interviewed Fan in late 2011, she asked to postpone our meeting to the early evening, as she had been notified that she had a place on a guided tour of the Beijing Municipal Environment Monitoring Centre. This was part of the Chinese government's recent initiative in promoting political transparency and disclosing government information. Although this guided tour was supposed to take place every week and be open to all, it was quite tricky to sign up for a place. First of all, it was open only to Chinese nationals. In addition, anyone who wanted to join the tour was required to complete an application form online, giving their national ID number. Applicants then had to wait to be invited. The timing was hard to predict, as it was at the discretion of the Environment Monitoring Centre whether there were sufficient applicants to justify running the tour each week. If there were only a few applicants one week, that week's open tour was cancelled and applications were rolled over to the following week. The tour took place in working hours, so applicants also had to arrange to have time off work, so it could be a while after their application before they were able to join the tour. Fan was quite satisfied with the tour, during which she was briefed on the varieties of pollutants the Beijing centre has been monitoring. 'It's good that, after feeling the public pressure, the environment authorities responded with a certain degree of openness.' But she was also concerned that the centre refused to disclose either the locations of pollutant monitoring spots or the data collected, as they were all 'for research use only'. Fan concluded her visit with a mixture of disappointment and determination: 'The more we know what kind of information the officials hold, the more we realise what we should have the right to know.'

The determination of air quality standards may be essentially a domestic issue, but in the case of China, it was intertwined with international exposure and foreign scrutiny, especially given the alternative data readings released by US Embassy in Beijing. We asked staff at Green Beagle how they perceived the embassy's contribution to the national campaign for clean air. One responded: 'We think it's good that the Americans are doing independent monitoring. In case one day, we [as home grown ENGOs] are banned from monitoring, as least we know they [the US embassy] can continue the publication of data.'

As the public concern about PM2.5 levels heightened, in the early summer of 2012 the Chinese government expressed two views regarding independent air monitoring, one concerning the Americans and the other on Chinese ENGOs. Both immediately drew criticism.

On June 5, World Environmental Day, China's Deputy Minister of Environmental Protection, Wu Xiaoqing, spoke at the State Council's press conference. He stated that 'certain consulates in China should respect China's law and stop publicizing non-representative information on air quality' (S. S. Wang, 2012). Wu further stated that the monitoring and release of national environmental data 'concerns the public interest, and is part of government's public rights. Publishing data without consent was a violation of international convention as well as an intervention in China's domestic politics' (S. S. Wang, 2012). Although he did not name a country, the comment was obviously directed at the US Embassy. The US Department of State spokesperson Mark Toner responded that this is 'a service provided for American citizens, the Americans who work in the Embassy community and live in China', thus it was not interfering with China's internal affairs (Toner, 2012).

Wu's statement on defending national sovereignty over environmental protection met with severe criticism in the popular media. Netease, one of China's largest online news portal sites, organised a series of special reports on the topic.[4] Its main introduction read, 'the categorisation [of the US Embassy's action] as illegal and not respectful of national sovereignty has backfired immensely ... the administrative monopoly over the collection and release of environment information requires us to be more vigilant'.[5] Another commentary published on Sichuan Online first corrected China's official stand by claiming that air quality control is a government 'obligation' (yiwu), rather than a 'right' (quanli) as Wu had claimed. It went on to argue that to some extent, '(The Chinese) public has a reason to thank the US Embassy for monitoring PM2.5', for it brought about more transparency to China's air quality data. It was rather the Ministry of Environmental Protection of China that should reflect on the situation, and avoid being 'the obstacle to social progress' (D. B. Jiang, 2012).

Just as the mainstream public response was in support of the US Embassy, it was reported in early July that in the newly proposed revision of China's 2009 Regulations Concerning Environment Monitoring, campaigns such as 'I Monitor the Air for My Country' might become illegal. This proposed revision read 'without obtaining official sanction, any work unit or individual cannot, through any means, publicise information concerning environmental monitoring' (MEP, 2009, article 81).

Key ENGOs involved in grassroots monitoring were keen to express their views in the media, welcoming state–society collaborations, and stressing to the government that 'it is better to steer than have a total ban' (Lv and Zhang, 2012). International experience was also used in arguing for a right to air information and to establish the importance of the non-governmental contribution in monitoring regional air quality. For example the Air de Paris Balloon installed by the French company Aérophile SA in the André Citroën park provided real-time reports on atmospheric pollution using its lighting system. And many regional air-quality monitoring programmes in Europe and North America have entrusted independent organisations with reporting

---

4 See <http://news.163.com/special/reviews/airmonitor0606.html>.
5 <www.news.163.com>.

local pollution levels, such as the KentAir network in England (Tong, 2012).

The Imagined Communities of Respiration

This section focuses on the emergence of a nation-wide campaign for clean air, but it is not the usual national campaign initiated by the government and fuelled by nation-state patriotism. The association of actors in the collective struggle for cleaner air in China seems to resemble an 'imagined cosmopolitan community' (Beck et al., 2013; L. Zhang, 2012). This term is drawn and extended from the work of Benedict Anderson (1983), and refers to a sense of solidarity founded on the conscious awareness that people are living through and affected by similar experiences and events as distant others. In this case it is an 'imagined communities of respiration', as grassroots organisations, foreign embassies, foreigners living in China and the Chinese government were connected by concern about breathing healthy air. ENGOs and the Chinese media largely sided with the Americans rather than the Chinese government. However, nationalism was not excluded from these imagined communities, as it provides a master rhetoric in mobilising the public. Indeed, it could be argued that the notion of 'my country' (*zuguo*) was not taken for granted, but was, through a collective working together towards a shared objective, re-established. To monitor the air for one's country, or rather the act of self-participation in a public affair, was a process of both reclaiming rights and reconditioning state–society relations.

There are at least three key points in comprehending how domestic ENGOs contribute to social change. First, air pollution has been a matter of fact in China for at least two decades. But it has increasingly been seen as a compelling problem in recent years through successive international exposures and obvious deficiencies and broken promises in the old political approach to answering public questions.

Second, it is worth highlighting that the nation-wide campaign was not fuelled by reaction to Western criticism, political agendas or empty patriotism. Rather, from the start it was substantiated by scientific data and collective research. It was a campaign that spoke empirical truth to power. This data-based strategy is important. As is also demonstrated in the next section, it is an indicator of the increasing maturity of Chinese ENGOS as well as an essential steering tool for them to exert impact both within and outside China. In addition, the fact of knowing your limits was also used as part of legitimacy building for the ENGOs, in the sense of serving as both a political justification to the government, and a pragmatic constructive force to society.

Third, although ENGOs and the grassroots campaign they promoted were not politically confrontational, they effectively formed a critical supervision of Chinese political accountability. The fact that the government was considering a possible ban on civil monitoring was perhaps the best evidence of its impact. After much societal criticism, this proposed ban seems to have been put aside by the government (H. Zhang, 2012). And at the time of writing this book, Green Beagle had already initiated other generic programmes of public participation in pollutant monitoring, such as detection of levels of heavy metal pollution (Wang Shuo, 2012).

'From the Soil' Revisited

If we were to look for anything that defined the 'Chineseness' of Chinese society, we would have to start from the soil. This was a most influential statement about China made by renowned social-anthropologist Fei Xiaotong during his study at the London School of Economics in the first half of the 20th century. The foundation of Fei's thesis was that since it had been an agricultural society throughout history, much of China's culture and social structure was rooted in the practice of husbandry. As captured by the title of Fei's most well-known book, it was a society construed 'from the soil' (Fei, 1948[1992]).

Less than a century later, much of Fei's thesis seemed increasingly to haunt contemporary China. For China seemed to have become a society that had been uprooted from the soil into the mid-air of economic development as the World's Factory. After more than a decade of urbanisation, more than half of the Chinese population are urban residents (X. M. Yang, 2011). Most farmers with a longing for prosperity have left their villages and become migrant workers on construction sites or factories along the east coast and around the Pearl River delta. In many rural areas, only children and the very senior remain to tend to the soil (Wang and Luo, 2012).

The detachment from traditional farming and the march towards industrialisation and a market economy constitute contemporary Chinese conceptions of progress and notions of a good life. In Chapter 2 we discussed how public educational events were aimed at provoking reflection on human–nature relations. This section makes a further argument that environmental protection is not just about environmental policies or industrial compliance, but also poses a challenge to society itself, as it inevitably inflicts sharp questions about prevailing social values. Consequently, the impact it makes is not limited to a particular set of rules, but also includes a reshaping of social norms. This is not unique to China, but it may be seen as more acute there than elsewhere, as the country has gone through such dramatic transformation over the last 60 years.

The making and consumption of Apple-brand IT products in China is one example. Stories about Apple's Chinese suppliers have made headlines in both Chinese and Western media for two main reasons. One is the working conditions in the factories, most notably those run by Foxconn, which were first exposed when a number of workers committed suicide under the stress of extremely long working hours and labour exploitation (Duhigg and Greenhouse, 2012). The other is the illegal dumping of waste water and gas, and the use of toxic materials which produce health hazards for both the workers and nearby communities (Landreth, 2011). In line with the ENGOs we interviewed, we are not concerned primarily with the labour disputes here, but focus on the environmental contamination. The illegal dumping from these supplier factories had a direct effect on the quality of crops and water, and thus a strong physical link to the welfare of Chinese people. However, as we shall see, ENGO initiatives to address the cause of this pollution initially caused much controversy and did not receive much support from the Chinese public.

In this section, we first illuminate the background of the Apple case. We then explain public attitudes and the rationales of the ENGOs, before setting out how the case developed and concluded. If the air-quality campaign was mainly about mass mobilisation to press for domestic political commitments, then the Apple case provides insights into the broader vision of grassroots ENGOs.

Open Information and the Silent Apple

Over the first decade of the 21st century, southern China increasingly became a global hub for manufacturing branded IT products for major internationals such as Apple, Nokia and Dell. IT product factories are known to be big polluters. They use gases which act as irritants, presenting possible health hazards for local populations. They also make use of heavy metals (for example copper, nickel and lead) whose waste discharge at levels over the authorised standards can cause severe water and soil pollution. A common phrase in Chinese is 'trash vegetables' (*laji cai*), referring to vegetation that has a high heavy metal content which could potentially lead to chronic intoxication, cancer and birth defects (J. Liu, 2012).

Chinese ENGOs' collective action against industrial illegal dumping was closely connected to one particular government reform: the political resolution to provide better public disclosure. Government information is often kept from the public for fear that it will be misused, because of its claimed irrelevance, or because its disclosure might cause political unrest. However, in the first decade of the 21st century, as an effort to increase government transparency, the State Council introduced the Regulation of the People's Republic of China on the Disclosure of Government Information, which took full effect on May 1, 2008 (State Council, 2007). In responding to this new political initiative, China's environment authority, the then State Environmental Protection Administration (now the MEP), was among the first to set out specific disclosure rules. The Measures for the Disclosure of Environmental Information (for Trial Implementation) were enacted on the same day (State Environmental Protection Administration, 2007). This provided a legal mandate for both government bureaus and enterprises to release environmental information. Chinese ENGOs as well as the mainstream media were keen to follow the enforcement of these new rules (Hu, 2010).

Moreover, ENGOs did not limit their actions to trying to ensure that the government kept its promises, but incorporated this new government commitment into their own agendas. For example, the leading ENGO in Beijing, the Institute of Public and Environmental Affairs (IPE), had been collecting publicly available data for years as part of its attempt to map out and trace water pollution sources.[6] The promulgation of the new open information regulation in 2008 largely extended its capacity for independent pollution monitoring. In a 40-minute special on China's Central Television, the director of IPE recounted that in 2009, IPE had turned its attention to heavy metal pollution. On basis of the records it had collected, IPE affirmed that illegal dumping by IT manufacturers was an increasing threat to the Chinese soil. On a closer examination, IPE further identified that most of these factories were suppliers to international brands.[7]

Conventionally, illegal discharge was often considered to lie within the vertical power relations between local government and the manufacturer in question. Yet increasingly the survival of manufacturing facilities depended not only on local approval but

---

6 <www.ipe.org.cn>.

7 <http://news.cntv.cn/china/20111030/106319.shtml>.

also on their performance and competitiveness within a horizontal supply chain. Thus it seemed that a more effective approach to the problem would be to pressure upstream brand companies to coordinate responsible supervision with their suppliers, and to incentivise contracted manufacturers to comply with environmental standards. Upon such reflection, 41 environmental groups in China formed the Green Choice Alliance[8] (hereafter the Alliance). The idea was to empower the public with a general awareness that they as consumers had the right and power to influence how their products were made.

Among the initial 29 international IT brands that the Alliance identified as having problematic Chinese suppliers, 28 responded with varying degrees of acknowledgement and/or commitment to reducing the pollution caused in their supply stream. There was only one exception: Apple Inc.

On April 15, 2010, the Alliance further reported to Apple on cases of illegal pollution discharge from companies believed to be its Chinese providers. Again, the Alliance had no response. The Chinese ENGOs carefully used the term 'suspected provider' (*yisi gonghuoshang*) to reflect a particularity of Apple Inc. That is, Apple regarded its global supply chain as a business secret and unlike other international corporations, refused to confirm who its subcontractors were. The list of its probable suppliers was drawn up using a combination of court evidence, stock information and news reports (FON, IPE and Green Beagle, 2011).

It was not until a month later, when a California-based NGO, the Pacific Environment (PE), followed up the Chinese ENGOs' enquiries, that Apple responded. PE had been promoting green activism in the Pacific Rim since the late 1980s.[9] One reason, among many others, for PE's attention to Chinese environmental protection is reflected in an alarming sentence on its China webpage: 'In the air above California, one quarter of the pollutants can be traced back to China'.[10] In other words, the concern of this California-based NGO about China's environment was self-interested as well as principled. Apple pledged to carry out an internal investigation, but made it clear that it would not disclose information to NGOs (FON, IPE and Green Beagle, 2011: 19–20).

During the summer of 2010, PE launched a campaign to

8 See <www.ipe.org.cn/alliance/ngo.aspx>.
9 See <www,pacificenvironment.org>.
10 See <http://pacificenvironment.org/section.php?id=183>.

encourage American consumers to join in pressuring Apple to be open about its investigation. According to PE, only after two weeks of launching the campaign, almost 1,000 letters had been sent by American consumers demanding 'a greener Apple' and for the company to 'agree to have a transparent discussion' with Chinese NGOs (X. M. Li, 2010).

In China, ENGOs strengthened their arguments for a greener Apple by producing more comprehensive evidence of the problems. After five months of field investigations, a coalition of Chinese NGOs released two environmental reports on Apple suppliers (for example Meiko Electronics, Kaedar Electronics, Unimicron Electronics and Foxconn) (FON, IPE and Green Beagle, 2011; FON et al., 2011).

But on the consumer front, although this initiative attracted much media attention worldwide and evoked consumer reaction in various countries, it met with resistance and scepticism within China. In fact a large section of the Chinese public suspected that IPE and the other ENGOs had intentionally singled out Apple to create a media stunt. Others, especially those young consumers who embraced Apple's brand culture, sided with Apple and criticised the Alliance's initiative as merely a way to avoid confrontation with local governments. It soon dawned upon Chinese ENGOs that to win support for their campaign, they not only needed to analyse the pollution statistics, they also had to understand and respond to the values held by domestic consumers.

A Clash of Values

The 'i' products launched by Apple, such as the iPod, iPhone and iPad, have undoubtedly been one of the biggest commercial success stories over the first decade of the 21st century. These products have revolutionised our personal and social behaviour in the digital age. For many the annual calendar revolves around Apple's spring and autumn product launches. The fanatical atmosphere at the Apple Macworld Expo and at every new product launch provides a good example of what Marx called 'commodity fetishism', in which society becomes enslaved by its own creations. A former Apple development engineer, Jim Reekes, said in the 2008 documentary *Welcome to Macintosh*, 'There is definitely a fanatical zealotry of Mac people. You know, um, it's not a religion. It's (rolling his eyes upwards) a computer.'

In China, Apple and its products have established cohorts of die-hard fans. On product release dates, there have been a few reported cases in which impatient Chinese customers used their fists and elbows to get to the front of the queue, where the chaos forced the temporary closure of stores (Wang, 2011; D. Wu, 2012). Within hours of Apple co-founder Steve Jobs' death on October 5, 2011, Weibo was flooded with more than 35,000,000 tweets (L. Zhang, 2011). Books about Jobs, especially translated versions of Walter Isaacson's biography, occupy prime shelf space in bookstores, supermarkets and shopping malls. In fact the nuanced differences between the traditional and simplified Chinese versions of Isaacson's biography were considered important by Apple fans in getting Jobs' legacy right (see Isaacson, 2011, 2012). For example, which translation best conveyed the true meaning and original aesthetics of Jobs' farewell letter to his wife was a topic of passionate debate on China's leading question-and-answer social networking website Zhihu (the Chinese equivalent to Quara). It is difficult, if not impossible, to think of a contemporary Chinese individual or brand that exerts a comparable fascination among the Chinese public.

One of our close friends was the founder of the earliest (and a highly influential) Chinese blog on Steve Jobs and Apple. In 2008, our friend took the trouble of registering its domain name in the United States, so as to have the blog domain appear as 'Apple4. us'. By 'us', he meant the Chinese. The aim of this blog, as he later explained, was to provide free and updated Chinese translations of Western reportage on Apple. The website was not simply a technical forum to inform Chinese readers of its latest product developments, but was also a channel to inspire a new generation of creativity.

From its 1984 'Big Brother' campaign, to the 'Lemmings' commercial, and the more recent 'Think Different' campaign, the Apple brand embodies the courage of standing up to power and challenging established norms. The brand story and the image of Jobs himself herald adventurous experiences. The commitment to provide the world with 'truly neat stuff' further suggests dedication, perfection and creativity (Belk and Tumbat, 2005). Thus, it is not surprising that Apple has a large community of admirers in a country which is known more for low quality, high political constraints, and a lack of a social and political enabling environment for originality (Deng, 2012).

In this context, it is perhaps not difficult to understand why direct criticism of Apple met with scepticism from Chinese consumers, especially amongst the younger generation who celebrated the values Apple claimed to stand for. For example, to make their arguments accessible to the public, ENGOs turned their investigations into Apple into two five-minute videos and made them available on major Chinese video sites, such as Tudou and Youku. There were more than half a million viewings of these two films. One of the videos began with a series of slides showing the joy and attachment of Chinese youth with Apple gadgets, with a caption reading 'Maybe you love Apple products, maybe you use Apple products, maybe you yearn to have Apple products, but do you know the story behind Apple?' The scene then switched to a satellite map. The lens zoomed out from the United States, rolled across the Pacific, and zoomed in to small towns in China, where 'suspected Apple suppliers' were based. The video showed branch streams of the Yangtze River turning into rivers of white thick substances moving through rural landscapes, and a small boy complaining about a weird smell in his village which gave him headaches and a nosebleed.

The reception for this film varied. One typical responder thought that the ENGOs were using Apple as the scapegoat for government incompetence, commenting, 'this has nothing to do with Apple, but is a failure of domestic law enforcement'. Even those who appeared to sympathise with the ENGOs' argument doubted the effectiveness of using upstream supply chain management to control industrial pollution: 'Apple is not unique regarding this [pollution]. Many other enterprises are the same. Thus can any real change be made? Even if you boycott Apple's product, wouldn't alternative products manufactured by other factories [cause] the same [pollution]?'[11]

However, in the eyes of Xiao Bai, director of the Nanjing-based ENGO Green Stone, direct public pressure on upstream companies was actually 'one of the most effective ways in solving real-world problems'. Green Stone made initial contact with IPE in 2009 and worked collaboratively with it to collect data on pollution stemming from the IT sector. In the absence of funding, Xiao Bai and her colleagues from Green Stone worked voluntarily.

Xiao Bai dismissed a popular criticism that Apple was a scapegoat for incompetent Chinese authorities, whom ENGOs were too timid to blame. For her, this was merely pragmatic thinking, as for ENGOs the best strategy was to confront the one with the greatest power to actually change the situation.

We never avoid contacting manufacturers, polluters, and local Chinese authorities themselves. But in this case, Apple Inc, manu-facturers, government as well as the consumers all have different responsibilities .... There is nothing wrong with us demanding

---

11 <http://v.youku.com/v_show/id_XMzAwNjE3OTY0.html>.

that Apple take up its responsibility. For manufacturers, between the government and the upstream buyer, it might be the upstream buyer that has a bigger power leverage that can demand conformity more effectively, as it directly reflects the manufacturer's economic interests. Thus it's not a matter of picking up the soft ones, but to pick up the one with actual leverage .... Plus, all these international brands are role models in their field. If all of them turn a blind eye to environmental consequences in their choice of suppliers, then we cannot even start to imagine what would happen to China's soil!

Thus, when all the brands they contacted gave a collaborative response except for Apple, Xiao Bai felt 'obligated to push things forward', for the economic leverage Apple had over its suppliers would provide incentives for compliance with environmental standards. It was also a matter of principle that the precedent should not be set of letting commercial giants outsource their environmental responsibilities. But she also knew she had a long way to go. A recent graduate, Xiao Bai was no stranger to the 'i'-products herself. She openly admitted that before she had discovered the linkage between Apple and the local contamination, she had been an admirer herself:

Before I saw the data on Apple suppliers' pollution in China, I was actually planning to buy a Mac. Because I'm also an amateur designer, and Mac suits my needs .... I see Apple as a maverick brand. Regardless of its high or low point, it sticks to its own belief and does not drift with the trend. That is really something. Plus, Apple is a really good design company, its design orientation is absolutely user-experience-based.

Despite her appreciation of Apple designs, in the fight against industrial pollution, Xiao Bai was also firm in pressuring Apple to take on its proper social responsibilities. Since 2011, she has acquired the nickname 'the Apple sister' (pingguo mei), because she has talked to people about Apple's environment responsibilities wherever she has gone. She has organised public events and engaged in one-to-one online discussions with sceptical Apple fans. She hoped other Apple supporters could also separate their admiration for Apple as an innovative icon from the need to urge the company to take its fair share of environmental accountability.

The ENGOs' reasoning that environment standards are best enforced by applying pressure through the transnational production chain was not unfounded. Research on corporate environmental management has confirmed 'a lack of effect of government pressure' in ensuring corporate environmental commitments. 'Societal pressure' was also found to be negatively associated with managerial motivation, as it is often not taken seriously. However, 'market-based incentives' were shown to be more effective in enforcing environmental regulations (Lo, Fryxell and Tang, 2010: 905; see also Economy, 2006).

In addition, financial considerations are a practical consideration for both subcontracted manufacturers and local government in the context of environmental protection. The 4S iPhone is a good example. Of its market price of $630, approximately $452, or 72 per cent of the market price, is gross profit for Apple. The Chinese manufacturers only get $7.10, or 1.1 per cent of the market price of each phone sold (Chakrabortty, 2012). The small profit made by the Chinese factories is reflected in the fact that there is fierce price competition to be awarded contracts with Apple.

While upstream companies shop globally for subcontractors, local authorities may also assist factories in these competitions to sustain local economic development. For example when Apple launch the iPhone 5 in 2012, Foxconn was required to increase its manufacturing capacity by recruiting 200,000 new workers so as not to disappoint would-be customers. Despite the damage to its public image from the workers' suicide cases, as a long-term Apple supplier, Foxconn remained a desirable economic driver to many local governments. In fact, to attract Foxconn to set up plants in Henan province, the provincial government sent out directives and a revised labour quota to all levels of state authorities as early as August 2012, so as to relieve part of Foxconn's hiring pressures. One incentive the provincial government offered for farmers to leave their land and join Foxconn's manufacturing plant was a monthly 200 RMB subsidy for every worker until the end of 2012. According to one estimation, this equalled a total of 1 billion RMB in government subsidies for persuading Foxconn to stay in Henan (Y. Liu, 2012).

Xiao Bai told us it was a challenge to persuade young consumers to consider 'the other side of Apple'. She felt frustrated from time to time, as she witnessed the contrast between the pollution victims, their barren crops, and excited young faces lining up outside Apple stores waiting to get the newest products. To some extent, she felt it was easier to collect pollution statistics and fieldwork data than to try to change this perspective gap between the two camps of her fellow Chinese.

Her colleague, Gao Teng, was more relaxed about 'convincing' Apple fans. She preferred the disputes: 'To have arguments means at least people start to pay attention to pollution and start to formulate their own opinions. The debate itself helps to clarify things and to popularise the idea of environmental protection.'

To be sure, the ENGOs' campaign did yield some results. The initial suspicion that the ENGOs had singled out Apple was gradually replaced by a more balanced reflection on the role of the company. For example, in October 2011 Huang Jixin, a visible figure in China's Apple user community, responded to a question regarding the appropriate share of environment accountability on Zhihu:

> [The pollution] has multiple causes. Fundamentally, this is a result of too high a local tolerance towards environmental pollution and [lack of] labour protection. If one looks further ... it is dereliction of duty of the government and non-action, which is directly linked to the lack of effective public supervision .... Should Apple be held accountable [for the pollution]? Yes, but it is not a [legal] obligation, it is a [social] responsibility .... According to Apple's 2011 Financial Report, its revenue is $10,825 billion USD, with a gross profit margin of 40.5%. With such a high profit margin, this is a company that can sacrifice part of its profit and allow its supplier factories to increase cost .... This is where media and NGOs should come in.[12]

While some Chinese Apple lovers may have recognised an ethical responsibility for Apple to supervise its suppliers, as Chinese ENGOs hoped for, the Chinese ENGOs were not able to generate visible Chinese consumer demand for a greener China, as their Californian partner PE had achieved with Western consumers. Fan Xiaqiu from Green Beagle, who participated in the compilation of the first Apple report, reckoned that this failure was a result of the public communication being trapped in the wrong frame:

> Somehow it seemed that we think Apple should have responded to us because other brands have. This was not the reason we went after Apple. We failed to communicate the idea of a green supply chain to a wider public. Most people still do not understand

---

12 See <www.zhihu.com/question/19848296>.

what it means. The key is to highlight that the environmental costs which appear at different stages of production may require a collaborative solution.

The point of seeking 'collaborative solutions', and exploring alternative channels to enforce environment compliance, perhaps never got across to the Chinese public. In fact, as we show in the following section, this campaign was more successful in getting organisational support from international NGOs and corporations.

A Greener Apple on the Ground

With international media exposure and pressure from ENGOs, in September 2011 Apple started a communication platform with Chinese NGOs, using a combination of telephone conferences and face-to-face discussions (Xie, 2011). In contrast to its earlier 'secretive' managerial style (FON, IPE and Green Beagle, 2011:19), in its *Supplier Responsibility Progress Report* published in January 2012, Apple not only noted that it had conducted 'specialized environmental audits at 14 suppliers in China' (Apple Inc, 2012: 16), it also publicised more than a hundred suppliers' names. In a follow-up to the *Responsibility Report*, a video conference was also held between Apple, the Natural Resources Defense Council in the United States and IPE in China. According to IPE, in this meeting Apple agreed to respect the standards set by China's Green Choice Alliance, and extend its coordination with green NGOs in its supervision of the supply chain.[13]

As of the time of writing of this book, Apple's environmental audits were still ongoing. Yet it seems safe to say that grassroots environmental actors have achieved clear influence. Chinese ENGOs' initiative on greening the transnational product chain also received applause internationally. Ma Jun, the director of IPE, was awarded the Goldman Environmental Prize in 2012, for his contribution to limiting environmental pollution by local and multinational companies operating in China, and for his 'most recent high-profile effort involving Apple'.[14]

To summarise the series of events regarding the Apple case as the story of an American multinational's pollution in China might be somewhat misleading. The social dynamic involved in the identification, negotiation and solution of the problem of illegal

---

13 See <www.ipe.org.cn/alliance/t_detail.aspx?name=??>.
14 <www.goldmanprize.org>.

discharges was not simply 'the Americans versus the Chinese'. Technically speaking, it was Chinese factories that created localised pollution through fulfilling their contracts on products to be consumed around the world. The two sides of the negotiation table might be better described as a cross-Pacific NGO coalition confronting a transnational supply chain.

It is worth noting that the two cases in this chapter took place during the same period, from 2009 to 2012. The key promoters of these two initiatives were also from an overlapping circle of green activists, especially the ENGO community in Beijing. In some cases, such as Fan Xiaqiu, the same individual was equally involved in both programmes. Corresponding to the three points made in analysing the nation-wide air monitoring programme, there are also three conclusions that can be drawn in understanding how ENGOs promoted changes within the social milieux they are in.

First, unlike the air pollution case, in which non-transparency and political inaction were regarded as the main hindrances to improving air quality, the causal interpretation for illegal dumping was seen as primarily rooted in (global) economic competition. Consequently the social milieu with which ENGOs identified was a transnational production chain. To some extent, whereas China's air pollution invoked international concern and ENGOs sought for domestic action, in the case of industrial contamination, it was a domestic problem that required international assistance in solving.

Second, whereas patriotism was at least employed as a rhetorical framework in legitimising the 'I Monitor the Air for My Country' program, the Apple case was a direct appeal to international responsibilities. Social actors started to establish new trans-local networks and break free from a conventional reliance on seeing nation-state regulation as the primary answer to social problems. But this does not mean an ignorance of the national context. In fact, ENGOs were innovative in synergising both national and global resources in pushing for local change. For example, the initial IT pollution report concerning 29 global brands was mainly a result of IPE in Beijing taking advantage of China's open information initiative. However, the eventual accomplishment of getting Apple's commitment to improve its record in China relied primarily on transnational collaborations with US-based NGOs.

Third, there was also a difference in the main vehicle employed to achieve environmental objectives. In the case of monitoring air quality, ENGOs soon established wide public support and were proficient in steering public participation into policy pressures. In contrast, in the case of Apple, ENGOs were more successful in gaining attention from commercial giants and winning assistance from global environmental communities. They failed to fully communicate their rationale to the Chinese public. Management studies often use the term 'global value chain' to capture transnational collaboration in the creation of economic goods, from design, production, and marketing to distribution and after-sale supports (Gereffi and Fernandez-Stark, 2011). To some extent, Chinese ENGOs were adept in instrumentalising the economic 'global value chain', but struggled in facing the other 'value chain' formed by globalised popular culture.

The argument we want to make for this chapter is a simple but often ignored one. It is that there is no single mindset or set formula to encapsulate how Chinese ENGOs set about their actions. The heterogeneities of framing problems, the versatility in pooling support, and the flexibility in seeking diverse solutions signify an important change for ENGOs working within a one-party state: the expanding notion of 'society'. In comprehending state–society relations in China, it is still easy to define where or how the 'state' is represented. But the conceptual boundary of society' has become evasive. It is a concept which no longer easily coincides with nation-state boundaries or collective historical memories. 'Society' has taken on a more real-time presence. In the cases presented here, social solidarities were established via causal interpretations of threats and responsibilities. As such, the conception of society expands geographically, into for example the 'trans-Pacific consumer society' in fighting industrial pollution. The idea of society also increases in its complexity, such as in the case of the 'imagined community of respiration' where both the United States and China view monitoring Beijing air quality as part of their 'domestic' responsibilities to citizens' health. While society becomes bigger and more intricately networked, how it is related to the state also changes.

4 CONFORMIST REBELS

The previous two chapters have demonstrated the significance ENGOs attach to environmental protection in contemporary China, and how environmental problems are framed and acted upon at the grassroots level. We have demonstrated how through public engagement, ENGOs have provided alternative ways of looking at environmental issues and have helped to expand the defence of environmental rights. However, while society is getting bigger, it does not necessarily mean that the government is getting smaller or weaker. Rather, the government is still the gatekeeper to vital resources in terms of both funding and information.

Therefore, to understand the limits of Chinese ENGOs and to make sense of their ambitions, it is important to look into how they situate themselves within the Chinese political context. That is, how do ENGOs perceive the role of the Chinese government and how do they relate their initiatives to government agendas? Bearing these questions in mind, this chapter makes a more direct examination of the relationship between the government and grassroots ENGOs.

Mitigating Administrative and Financial Constraints

Unregistered But Not Underground

Since the late 1990s, the Chinese government has, within limits, encouraged civil groups to address issues it has been unable to solve. The main prerequisite for this support is that such groups adhere to the principle of state leadership and register with the government (Frolic, 1997). However, NGO registration in China is notoriously difficult. This barrier of legal recognition not only applies to environmental protection, but can also be found to limit civil activities in other fields. Our previous research in the health sector indicated a similar difficulty for grassroots interest groups. For example, one of the better known health-related NGOs in China is the New Sunshine Foundation, a leukaemia patient rights group founded in 2002 by Liu Zhengchen. Liu himself was diagnosed with leukaemia during his study at Peking University. At the onset Liu's organisation, like many NGOs in China, was only recognised as a 'level-two' society at Peking University. This meant that the organisation was not recognised by Chinese law as a fully independent body carrying legal rights and responsibilities. Despite the fact that Liu's organisation enjoyed a high media profile and was praised for 'inspiring youth' by the Central Commission of the China Communist Youth League, it still took Liu and his colleagues seven years to obtain full legal status as an independent social organisation from Beijing's Civil Affairs Bureau (J. Y. Zhang, 2012: 172—5). In short, acquiring official recognition as a NGO can be an arduous process which takes years, no matter what field the group works in.

Yet this administrative barrier has not discouraged the bottom-up formation of NGOs. In fact, among the underground ENGO activists we interviewed, few were worried about not having official recognition from the government. Teng Anyu, founder of the natural photographic ENGO discussed in Chapter 2, told us that, similarly to what Liu had gone through, she was first advised to find a state-run institution to act as the supervising agency. After inquiring about the usual process of obtaining official recognition, she decided to remain underground:

> We are a small NGO with limited resources. Not to register with the Civil Affairs Bureau means we no longer need to find a supervising institution. We can save all the bureaucracy of being overseen by a superior institution and there would be no issues of making compromises. In short, we don't have a 'mother-in-law'. We are on our own. So long as we are happy to bear the risk, we can go ahead with any agenda.

Compared with being subject to control and having to compromise, escaping the difficulty of obtaining legal status seemed almost 'liberating'. Our work shows it has become the norm rather than the exception for small civil groups, unable to afford the time and labour to get state certification, to not register. However, many groups were quite relaxed about slipping into this legal grey area. The supposed constraints of being overseen by a 'mother-in-law' effectively no longer applied to these organisations. This had the benefit of yielding more autonomy in their choice of agendas. Cao Qing, a staff member working for another underground NGOs focusing on green agriculture and food safety, gave a similar view:

'We are an unregistered organisation, the government does not regulate us. Thus in most of our activities, we receive no support or opposition from the government.'

To refer to these unregistered NGOs as 'underground' NGOs may be somewhat misleading. They are neither seen as illegal nor are their operations as secretive as some other underground activities in China, such as underground artists, underground churches and underground abortion clinics. Despite the absence of an official status, many unregistered ENGOs, such as Teng's popular photographic training programmes, often run very much 'above ground'.

This 'unregistered but not underground' mindset is revealing. It indicates that, at least in the eyes of grassroots actors, the government only has limited significance and dominance in organising civil initiatives. For many, state approval was considered as an 'additional' rather than an essential accreditation for bottom-up projects.

Apart from the issue of legal paperwork, a more practical challenge of not registering is to secure financing. This difficulty is not limited to unregistered ENGOs, which obviously do not have the legal status to conduct public fundraising, but also presents a constraint to most licensed NGOs. This is because there is no almost no public funding apart from government channels (Economy, 2005; Tang and Zhan, 2008). However, as discussed in the following section, this situation began to change around 2010. In the words of one activist, domestic ENGOs started to explore alternative ways of pooling funds and tackling this constraint creatively.

Conceptual Labour with Real Cash

'China does need reforms. But that does not mean that before the system is changed, we should just wait and do nothing.' In a warm spring afternoon in Beijing, we met with Mu Shuihe on the huge balcony of his ENGO headquarters. He added:

The most effective way of promoting environmental causes is to play by the government's rules as much as possible and beat government regulation at its own game. Of course, if you push for grassroots initiatives, you will confront many constraints in China. And you will not be as free and or legally protected as civil groups in the West. But, once you're out there pushing for changes, you find there is still much that can be achieved. You just have to act creatively.

One of the biggest constraints confronted by Chinese ENGOs is financial backing. It is a well-known fact that in the absence of sustained domestic funding, ENGOs in China are 'highly reliant on either personal funding of the NGO founders (leaders) or international funding' (Tang and Zhan, 2008: 434). In many academic research papers, Chinese environmentalists are mainly described as 'intellectual-activists' with a 'well-educated urban' background or from 'social and political elites' (Ogden, 2004; Yang, 2009; Tang and Zhan, 2008). In the Chinese public imagination, however, ENGO staff are seen less as social and political elites, and are closer to environmental crusaders. That is, they are strong-minded, self- (or even family-) sacrificing individuals who live on the high moral ground, coping with a chronic shortage of funds (Feng, 2010).

The general image of impoverishment presents a serious problem for the growth of ENGOs. That is, how can they hire and maintain qualified staff? The level of personal income is a pragmatic concern in China, a country with effectively no social safety net. Most citizens depend on their own income to pay for education, housing and healthcare. This is especially the case for the generation born after the one-child policy. As they enter the workforce, they also carry the burden of providing for their parents' retirement care. The 4–2–1 problem is well established in China: four grandparents, two parents, and only one child to take care of them as they age.

During our research, we contacted two high-profile student environmental groups, one in the southwest of China and the other in the northeast. Most students we talked to were very dedicated and passionate about their regional environmental protection programmes. They included wetland preservation, trash recycling, saving Tibetan antelopes and campaigns about acid rain. But almost all of them showed reluctance when we asked if they would consider working for an ENGO after graduation. Chen Feifan, a biology student, described working for domestic NGOs as a 'luxury':

> Most NGO jobs are poorly paid and very demanding as well. My parents and relatives wouldn't understand. Plus, as the only child, I feel I also have the responsibility of being financially well-off so that I can take care of my parents. For me that's a reality and a priority. I'd love to continue to contribute to environmental causes and I'm sure I will, regardless of what my job will be after leaving university. But for me, working for an ENGO, especially a domestic one, is purely a luxury.

Even among the full-time ENGO staff we met throughout China, a good portion of those under 35 confessed that they were likely to opt for other professions later in their lives. One example is a senior staff member working for a southern ENGO. Despite her passion about the environment, she considered it would only be natural to 'move on' to a better-paid job after devoting a few years in ENGOs:

> Don't get me wrong, I enjoy my current job. I think environmental protection will always be part of my life. But I don't see my whole career here. For me, working for ENGOs provides a big platform and I will move on. Because, of course there are practical personal situations to think about too, such as having a family and getting settled.

We asked her what kind of work she thought she could get after leaving the ENGO sector. She responded:

> Oh, lots, working for the corporate social responsibilities sector of industries, consulting companies or other choices too. I might even seek a scholarship and retrain abroad. Many of my predecessors on this post ended up in a diversity of fields and succeeded. They still come back and contribute to our programme designs and bring us fresh ideas from different sectors. I want to be like them.

In short, both the prospective and current members of ENGOs share a similar rationale. That is, ENGOs are a sort of stepping stone on the way to a respectable job to finance their private responsibilities and fulfil other social expectations.

Thus, back to that sunny balcony in Beijing, when Mu was talking about 'acting creatively' and having to act within the law to beat the constraints set by government regulations. Zhang immediately pointed to the busy office inside, and asked him, 'How did you afford all these people? Are they are volunteers?' There were at least eight people working at the residential flat converted into an office. Everyone was occupied: making phone calls, documenting samples or typing at the computer. 'They are all paid employees, some full time, some part-time', Mu said proudly.

> We used Taobao [the Chinese equivalent of ebay] to raise some of our staff's salaries. You see, the government has so many restrictions on public fundraising, but it does allow you to set up an

account on an ecommerce site and sell products. So our organisation set up an account, and we have goods too. But our product is 'conceptual'. It's our service on environmental protection. So we don't deliver through postal boxes but through our work. People can buy our 'product' online, and the money will then be turned into our staff salaries.

Mu's organisation was not the first ENGO we encountered that raised funds through Taobao. When we were researching another ENGO in Beijing, we also found a Taobao link on its main website. The Taobao account had only one product on offer: a framed photographic work that cost 150 RMB. The photo was of mediocre quality and 150 RMB was obviously too high a price. What was more surprising, we noticed that about a dozen prints had successfully been sold. When we later got in touch with this ENGO and inquired how they calculated the price for this photographic work, the person in charge explained:

> Ah, it wasn't about the photo. It was how much it cost per person for a field trip we organised. It included the fuel and travel insurance. It was an open event so we asked anyone who wanted to join to pay directly online. It makes things easier and more reliable than handling cash on an individual basis.

While legal public fundraising is subject to tight regulations, Chinese ENGOs employ the internet as a channel to fund events as well as salaries. Using Taobao as an alternative source of funding is a recent occurrence among Chinese ENGOs. Mu's organisation was able to offer a monthly salary of 3,000 to 8,000 RMB. To be sure it was still hard work. 'In here, each person needs to take on several roles', one of Mu's employees told Zhang. The employees joked that they had to function like characters in the American comic series *Transformers*. For any given project, they needed to take whatever role was required: the organiser, the coordinator, the contact or even the driver. But at least the salary on paper was a lot more competitive than a few years ago, and this may help to retain some talents in ENGOs.

Chinese ENGOs were sensitive to new options. Currently, a few ENGOs were exploring the new online event management platform Youfu (yoopay.cn) as a better tool to finance public events. More important, the concept of crowd-funding has just been introduced to China, giving rise to websites such as Dianming Shijian (demohour.

com). Modelled on the peer-to-peer micro-lending platform that first emerged in the United States, these websites connect personal or collective small-budget projects that normally do not have institutional funding sources with individual donors. Individuals upload audio and visual descriptions of the proposed project, accompanied with the expected outcome and required budget. Interested members of the public donate whatever amount they choose. Together, a number of these small donations may amount to the budget required. The funders only receive non-financial returns from the recipient. This not only provides ENGOs with new channels to support their ideas, it also further liberates them from government domination of social resources. As one interviewee put it, 'Everyone will become the reviewer, funder and supervisor of civil initiatives.'

The Symbiotic Relationship with Government

Although most ENGOs devote much energy to mitigating the effect of the administrative and financial constraints set by the government, few environmentalists we interviewed saw the relationship between ENGOs and the Chinese government as antagonistic. In fact, as is discussed in this section, almost all of them saw the government as a key actor in achieving a green society, and ENGOs were keen to develop diverse channels of collaboration. A previous study on the grassroots transformation of China's politics indicated that relations between the government and civil actors should be seen as 'symbiotic and co-operative, conflicting and compromising, rather than binary and opposite, coercive and submissive' (Gui, Ma and Muhlhahn, 2009: 417). Our research supports this finding. ENGOs looking at the government's role in promoting environmental protection saw the state as neither monolithic nor static. Rather, they were both diplomatic and pragmatic in steering political institutions' executive power into green initiatives.

The Government's Role Viewed from the Bottom Up

A common characterisation of Chinese homegrown NGOs is that they are 'often not very adversarial or confrontational' (Mol and Carter, 2006: 160; Yang, 2005; Lu, 2007). As demonstrated in this section, our findings concurred with this view. However, it would be wrong to equate a non-confrontational attitude with being submissive or passive. In fact, most grassroots activists we interviewed were contemplative and tactical in locating the government's role in promoting a green society. One example was Song Kai, an environmentalist in her mid-40s currently managing a small ENGO in Beijing. When we asked her what she considered key in pushing for changes in China, Song replied pragmatically, 'There are two must dos: one is to follow a "populist path" (qunzhong luxian) and the other is to attend to your relationship with the government. It is all about getting the common people as well as the government to support your views.' Song went on to explain her view:

It's like participating in a chess match. The government's aim is about 'winning' the chess of development. The key to winning is to set out the right combination of moves rather than about saving individual pieces. It's not so much that the government has not recognised or doesn't know what it is sacrificing. But for some issues, it doesn't consider it a priority. And the bureaucracy considers that these losses are justified – although it may not be reasonable at all – as these losses contribute to the long-term goal of winning the game. Thus, the role of grassroots organisations is to make sure any sacrifice is absolutely necessary and is reduced to the minimum.

In the eyes of Song Kai, ENGOs should form a watchful alliance with the government and exercise advisory oversight over governmental actions. For Song, the underlying assumption is that both ENGOs and the state share an interest in pursuing social prosperity, or 'winning the chess match'. As such, there are no fundamental sources of adversity between the two parties. Thus, ENGOs should 'attend to' their relationship with the government and 'participate in' the match – that is, influence its strategies. This alliance should also be watchful, as the government may have different ideas of 'the right scheme' and different measures of justification. ENGOs should stick closely to the interests of the society, and guard against the false rationality of bureaucracy and making avoidable sacrifices for political glory. In short, the government may be the main movers of the 'chess pieces' but ENGOs ensure there is a critical examination of what has been lost and what has been gained.

This recognition of overlapping interests, and their potential to lead to collaborative rather than adversarial relations, is not just a one-sided wish. It is also reciprocated by the government. In recent years, a number of civil activists have taken on government advisory roles at various levels. In an attempt to 'gradually introduce and refine public participation systems in environment protection', in June 2000 the then State Environmental Protection Administration made 40 special appointments of leading environmentalists in China to be its 'environment envoys' (*huanjing shizhe*) (Chen, 2000). The appointments included representatives from core groups of environmentalists, such as Liang Congjie (Friends of Nature), Tang Xiyang (Green Camp) and Wang Yongchen (Green Earth Volunteers). However, the actual scope of political participation these envoys were entitled to remained unknown. But as Zhu Can, a programme officer working at the Beijing office of an international ENGO, pointed out, a more common way of promoting environment agendas in China is through establishing organisational 'partnerships' with the government:

A major difference between doing environment protection in China and in the West is that, in the West, many civil organisations are empowered and have the capacity to promote an idea on their own. In China, for various reasons, you still need to run things by the government to make progress. In other words, you need to find a local partnership (*dangdi de hezuo huoban*). I think people working in NGOs all know that, if you want to get things done, the tacit rule is for each partner to know their role. Even within the NGO communities, we also need to collaborate over what different NGOs can do. For example, domestic NGOs are best at identifying grassroots problems but international NGOs may possess more professional capacity. It's not about a simple binary of Westernisation versus localisation. We just need to tailor the approach to suit our goal.

Providing advisory oversight to existing rules and seeking collegiality on new initiatives may not be mutually exclusive, but may be two overlapping objectives in some ENGO programmes. Huang Wei, an ENGO staff in her late 20s working on trash recycling programmes in urban residence areas, provides an example. When she was hired, her job description included compiling policy research reports and communicating with relevant government offices. But though her work, she started to see the Chinese government as the organisation's biggest client.

Much of what the NGOs are doing is to fill in the gaps in government responsibilities. Of course, unless China has an extremely huge civil servant body, it won't reach every residential community and every small vein of the society. It would cost a lot and administratively it is not realistic either. Social organisations have the flexibility to spot needs and respond to them. This is a bottom-up process. If the government likes what we do and recognises it does not have the capacity to accomplish it, then the government can purchase our service.

To summarise, domestic ENGOs did not simply see the Chinese government as an overarching political power. In the examples above, the government was recognised as a general commander in social development, a resourceful partner to enforce new green programmes and a potential client that may finance environment projects with mutual benefit. The role of the government was not conceptualised as wielding hegemonic power, but was projected through diverse angles. This is important as it reveals the scope and dynamics of ENGOs' interactions with the state. But if it was the political economic system promoted by the government that led to environment problems in the first place, how did engaging the government work in achieving ENGOs' objectives?

Attaching the Government's Name

Since ENGOs represent an alternative social force in overseeing political power, and since they operate under many constraints, we found it natural to assume that in many of their collaborations with the government, ENGOs might be protective of their share of public recognition. On learning our theory, one former WWF programme officer, Kang Yuanyou, who had worked closely with various local Chinese authorities, laughed. He said that of course ENGOs were careful about maintaining their independence and neutrality, but there was no popularity contest. In fact, more often than not, Kang and his colleagues were only 'too happy to see the local government take all the credit'.

Kang used the example of introducing new green initiatives in China. The main workload for him and his colleagues normally started with substantial background research, so that they would have hard data and persuasive arguments to get relevant government offices and other stakeholders interested. This could be an arduous process, which involved several rounds of communication and coordination with various local parties. Eventually, their idea might start to put down roots among the locals, and there might be a press conference or a formal publication to mark the local commitment to this new initiative:

> After all the hard work, of course we would be happy to see our name appear on the publications alongside the local government. But it would be better if the government totally forgot about us, and framed it as if it was their own initiative and their own idea. Because that means an ENGO initiative has transformed into a government commitment. This is important, because even international NGOs can rarely sustain a long-term operation at any particular location. The best scenario is to pass on the torch to local institutions. Thus, we are relieved and delighted to see that local authorities take on the project as their own. As long as the initiative is adopted, our goal is achieved. My colleagues and I are quite happy to stay behind the scenes. In fact, I'd have a heartfelt giggle at seeing our names missing.

Zhu Can shared a similar rationale. In pushing for clean air initiatives in Chinese cities, Zhu and his colleagues would always seek joint publication of their project findings with relevant local authorities: 'It was only when local government considered something not yet appropriate that we went on to publish reports in our own name.'

At a glance, it almost seemed that ENGOs were been taken advantage of and were being left behind the scenes. On a closer look, this accreditation of authorship to the government was not simply a generous act of sharing political credits, but it was also an extension of liability for the project concerned. As such, to welcome government bodies attaching their names to reports and projects was to welcome a sharing of commitments. This point was further expanded by Huang Wei, who, relating to her work on trash recycling, said that for a project to bear the name of a government body also facilitates the institutionalisation of new practices:

> For NGOs, the point of departure is reason, we try to gradually steer people to rational and sensible choices. But for the government, it has the advantage of implementing laws and administrative regulations, which carry a binding force with immediate influence on people's well-being. Take the sorting of domestic rubbish for example. We can let the residents see that this is a good thing to do, but we have to rely on the local

government as well as the resident committee (*juweihui*) to institutionalise such a practice.

Thus getting the government onboard may enable the translation of 'should-dos' into 'must-dos'. The working relations between ENGOs and the government described by the three interviewees quoted above seemed almost like a relay race. ENGOs run the initial distance of locating the problem and working out possible solutions, then they are happy to have the government take over the baton. At least two insights can be drawn from such framing of ENGO–state relations. One is the underlying rationale of how a green society in China can be achieved. The encouraging attitudes towards administrative involvement from government at all levels seem to suggest that, in the eyes of ENGOs, what Chinese society needs is not a rebellion against the rules but efforts to amend and (re)institute the forces of law and order. Relatedly, the second insight is into how a green government can be achieved. It may seem an oversimplification to say that Chinese ENGOs avoid confrontations with the government, since as previous chapters have demonstrated, environmental activists are not shy in bringing forward contentious issues and are firm in demanding responses. But most of these initiatives are problem-focused. Therefore, it may be more accurate to say that Chinese ENGOs avoid confrontation over abstract ideals, but set out to change government practice through grounded environmental solutions. These two points are now examined in turn.

First, given the facts that most Chinese ENGOs have been pushed into operating in a legal grey area and need to act creatively to relieve their financial constraints, they might not appear as likely candidates to promote the rule of law. However, observers of Chinese ENGOs have noted that in the past few years, 'we see that grassroots ENGOs are also starting to take advantage of national laws and regulations, and "follow the procedures" (*zou chengxu*) in all circumstances' (Feng, 2009: 185).

As was exemplified in Chapters 2 and 3, a shared theme of many high-profile environmental campaigns is their reliance on the enforcement of the law (for example in the protection of the Kekexili NNR), the exercise of legal rights and the demand for controls (for example in civil monitoring and the Apple case). Note that in the Kekexili protection case, the key argument Wang Zhen used to stop Snow Beer was not the ethical point about human–nature relations, but an explicit suspicion that the company had violated the State

Council's Regulation on Nature Reserves (1994). Wang and his friends did not resort to disruptive demonstrations; instead he created a sphere of 'public gaze' that demanded a response from Snow Beer. In the civil monitoring initiatives, although Chinese ENGOs acted as an alternative source for producing and disseminating air monitor statistics, their action was not aimed at establishing a rival authority that would compete with existing ones. In fact, the limits of civil monitoring were carefully emphasised throughout the campaigns over air quality and other urban pollution issues. The objective was to enforce better codes of practice in professional institutions, and improve the transparency and public accountability of the government. The exercise of rights and demands for controls were more apparent in the Apple case. The initial IT industry pollution report was a demonstration of making use of every citizen's entitlement to information. The aim of the Apple campaign was to instil order and control into the global production chain. In short, grassroots actors were not acting in defiance of authorities. Quite on the contrary, they exerted influence by following the rules of the game, and in the process, improved those rules.

Second, it may be useful to recall that for most ordinary people living in China, environmental issues are increasingly being felt at a personal level. There is an acute sense of urgency because people experience real problems. Thus, the interest of ENGOs in engaging with the government and promoting problem solving is not simply to reduce friction with the government, but is also a pragmatic way of acquiring social support and establishing authority. As one environmentalist in Gansu told us, 'we want the public to see that we are here to help, rather than to make trouble (daoluan)'.

In this sense, previous studies are right in suggesting that 'the "political room" for a western-style environmental movement' is 'limited' in China (Mol and Carter, 2006: 160). However, this is neither to say that the Chinese environmental movement will always remain problem-oriented and largely devoid of ideological debate, nor to discredit the changes ENGOs have brought to China. Getting the government involved in previously neglected societal issues and improving institutional behaviour are important aspects of political reform. While society is becoming more rights-conscious, and starting to demand the rule of law, existing Chinese institutions may also be pressured to change.

On this account, China has much historical global experience to refer to. Former environmental movements in Eastern Europe socialist countries in the 1980s demonstrated how ecological issues function as an alternative channel for greater political freedom and the empowerment of civil society (van der Heijden, 1999; Sarre and Jehlicka, 2007). In her study of ENGOs in south-west China, Caroline Cooper (2006) made an interesting comparison between the formation of civil society in contemporary China and green movements in Poland and Hungary a few decades ago. Cooper demonstrated that similar to the experience of Eastern European societies, environmental protection provides 'a pliant entry point' for Chinese grassroots to exert political influence (Cooper, 2006: 134). The symbiotic relations between the state and society in China were captured as the 'local state associational model' which presents 'a tenor of state accommodation of civil society, and civil society actors are seeking to expand this through securing creative legal registration and defending the space allocated by the state' (Cooper, 2006: 113–14). Should a greener future be entrusted to a bigger civil society or a stronger government? For the Chinese, this may not be an either/or choice, but a both/and solution.

ENGOs: A Rebel and a Conformist

Much research on Chinese ENGOs has centred on the emergence of civil society and the extent of its political impact in an authoritarian state (Ma, 2003; Yang, 2005; Cooper, 2006; Gui, Ma and Muhlhahn, 2009; Lu, 2007). In summarising China's state–ENGO relations, one sociologist in Beijing, who has written extensively on China's environmental issues in the 2000s, concluded that the government is 'the lead actor' (*zhujue*), while the ENGOs are 'supporting actors' (*peijue*). This evaluation, he told us, was based on how environmental protection historically developed in China:

China's environmental movement had a very different start from the West. In Western countries, the environmental movement started with civil society and mainly followed the footsteps of the civil rights movement and feminist movement. But in China, it was the government that initiated environmental actions. The civil reactions were initially not about resistance [to government]. It was more like the society catching up with the government. So China's civil environmental organisations are only supporting actors.

To be sure, there remains a substantial gap between the executive capacities of the Chinese government and the domestic ENGOs.

However, after two decades of development, the relationship between ENGOs and the government may need to be revisited. There is still much truth in seeing the government as lead actor and ENGOs as supporting actors. But how government 'leads' and how ENGOs 'support' green initiatives in China may require some unpacking. The government's perspective on the environment is discussed in the next chapter. In this chapter, it is demonstrated that ENGOs did not take the government's role uncritically and did not leave government regulations unchallenged.

To begin with, the relations between ENGOs and the government are multilayered. Most ENGOs were not discouraged from the high bar of being legally recognised by the government, for government was not seen as the authority in legitimising their activities. Rather, ENGOs framed the roles of government institutions from a utilitarian orientation: that is, in terms of their financial, executive, legislative and managerial contributions to proposed projects. For more than two decades, much research has noted how controlled encouragement and careful cultivation of a non-government sector constitute part of Chinese government's strategy in instrumentalising civil actors (Whiting, 1991; Schwartz, 2004; Moore and Warren, 2006). Instead of the domination of a top-down command from government authorities, there seemed to be a bottom-up instrumentalisation of the government.

The ENGOs have used a combination of strategies to try to mitigate the constraints set by the government. Studies on European and Australian environmental groups have suggested four common campaign strategies, which can all be found in Chinese ENGOs:

- information sharing and public awareness raising
- participatory or persuasive political lobbying
- confrontational legal action
- a 'working together' ethos encouraging networked contributions.

Furthermore, research suggests that ENGOs rarely confine themselves to only one type of approach, but rather appear to be both 'revolutionary' and 'reformist' at the same time (Richards and Heard, 2005; Hall and Taplin, 2007). The key reason for ENGOs' flexibility of role play is, similarly to Chinese environmentalists' concerns, to 'break out of the environmental ghetto' and reach out to the wider society (Hall and Taplin, 2007: 103). In this sense, Chinese ENGOs are no different from their Western counterparts.

What is particular to the Chinese case, however, is that it was a country with little tradition of civil society that has relied more on administrative commands than the enforcement of law. Chinese homegrown ENGOs may be 'intra-system operations' in the sense that they do not challenge the political legitimacy of the government, but they need to think outside the box in bringing their ideas into fruition. By trying to 'beat the government at its own game', homegrown ENGOs are rebels and conformists at the same time. As demonstrated in the previous chapter, they have expanded the circle of environmental discourse to the wider public and explored new forms of public participation. They have also emphasised keeping to the rules. They have encouraged the public not just to be informed of what is promised by law, but also to become accustomed to exercising and defending their rights. Taking these points into account, it could be said that ENGOs have greatly increased both the volume and weight of Chinese civil society within the existing political framework.

5 THE GREEN LEAP FORWARD

For most Chinese in the late 1950s the Great Leap Forward was neither great nor a leap forward. It represented a near-perfect example of irrational instrumentality, as everything was calculated and organised to achieve a specific end – to catch up and surpass the industrial powers by boosting national iron and steel production and producing enough food to not only feed China but to export to others as well. Many Chinese who lived through that time recount the amateur 'backyard furnaces' which were set up in people's communes to support the effort. In places, even cooking woks and door knobs were brought from work units and individual homes to be melted down to make high-grade steel. But this collective zealousness was also highly irrational, as while much calculation had been done on the means to achieve the ends, there seemed to be little room for reflecting on the end itself. Was making steel the real indicator of industrialization? Was the race to meet production targets a numbers game or did it meet actual needs? When people enthusiastically melted away their goods, they returned home only to realise there was no wok to cook dinner with, and as time wore on, no food to cook either. The not so Great Leap Forward resulted in as many as 45 million deaths as a result of famine, poor planning, and murderous campaigns of ideological purity (Dikotter, 2010).

So with contemporary China's increasing thirst for energy, its poor environment and its alarming income gaps, there is little doubt that the country is in need of a 'great green leap forward' to usher society onto a better developmental track. This time coal conversion will replace backyard furnaces, targets will focus on greenhouse gas emissions rather than production quotas, and the guiding ideology will be sustainability, not socialism. But in a similar vein to critics of the first Leap, we need to ask: Does higher solar panel production really mean a greener China? Do increasing numbers of wind turbines necessarily indicate a low-carbon economy? Does being the largest host of CDM projects equate to dominance in carbon markets? In a sense, perhaps the worries expressed by Chinese climate sceptics in Chapter 1 may indicate more prescient questions than first seemed to be the case.

In previous chapters we have explored China's ENGOs. We now turn to the dominant actor in China's green politics, the government. We finish, rather than start, the book with this chapter in keeping with our view that more needs to be done to emphasise and support the role of Chinese civil society, and the many ways in which it participates in the public deliberation over environmental issues. In this chapter, we outline the benefits and drawbacks of China's political system, and discuss the ways in which government is on side with the ENGOs' agenda. We cite examples from the 12th Five Year Plan, focusing on the notion of a circular economy and the growth of eco-cities. We end by discussing the wider socio-political context of China's green movement, and what the Party's hopes of creating a 'harmonious ecological civilisation' tell us about the state of Chinese politics today.

'Policies from Above and Countermeasures from Below'

Much of the English-language literature on Beijing's role focuses on the authoritarian nature of the government. This can be seen through the two most cited phrases used to describe Chinese environmental governance: 'fragmented authoritarianism' and 'environmental authoritarianism'. In many ways, these labels have nothing to do with environmental politics as such. Rather they describe the perception of a government known for demanding complete obedience to its own authority at the expense of individual freedom. Yet, as we shall see, these labels are not necessarily pejorative and do not reflect wholly negative judgments.

Indeed, many who employ the term 'environmental authoritarianism' not only wish to describe how China is responding to environmental challenges but also prescribe a model for how it (and others) *should* effectively respond (Gilley, 2012; Beeson, 2010). There is some debate, which we will not rehearse in detail here, over whether or not an authoritarian system is better able to cope with environmental problems than a democratic regime, given the extent to which the latter are often bogged down in indecision, opposition politics, and the need to please electorates every four years (Shearman and Smith, 2007).

Environmental authoritarianism refers to a policy process that is dominated by a relatively centralised state. It posits that an enlightened group of elites hold sole responsibility for making and implementing environmental policies. Non-government actors are expected to participate in state-led campaigns in order to implement decisions, but only a small number of technocrats are engaged in actually making those decisions. The advantage to an authoritarian model is that government responses to environmental crises can, in theory, be quick and comprehensive, thus affording greater chance of achieving the intended results. This is often achieved through a loss of individual liberty that prevents individuals from engaging in unsustainable behaviour and compels them to obey environmentally friendly policies – though again, even a casual observer would recognise that in actual practice this trend is highly uneven. Nonetheless, in acting in this way, governments tend to co-opt environmental movements, making them tools of their own, and potentially helping to boost their legitimacy by pointing to a green-friendly rhetoric and record of environmental protection (Gilley, 2012).

While China clearly fits this description, a number of other countries, notably Singapore, are also cited as prime examples. Environmental authoritarianism has some surprising advocates. Vaclav Havel, for example, wrote in the *New York Times* several years ago, 'I don't agree with those whose reaction is to warn against restricting civil freedoms. Were the forecasts of certain climatologists to come true, our freedoms would be tantamount to those of someone hanging from a 20th-storey parapet' (Havel, 2007).

However, in the case of China, if environmental authoritarianism helps to push through green initiatives, then fragmented authoritarianism helps to ensure that the impact of those initiatives is less than was hoped. Since it was first proposed in the 1980s, the fragmented thesis has remained the most influential model of Chinese governance (Lieberthal and Oksenberg, 1988; Lieberthal, 1992). In brief, it asserts that policy made at the centre becomes increasingly malleable as it trickles down. It is worth exploring this concept in some detail.

The origins of the fragmented authoritarian model lie in Deng Xiaoping's reforms, which gave more authority and responsibility for resource allocation to provincial governments. Unlike the Maoist years, where national campaigns and Party concerns filtered down into virtually every level of society, since the Reform era, the central government has enjoyed much less control over the provinces. Deng's reforms included a decentralisation of budgetary decision making, the reduced use of political coercion, and a decline in the use of political ideology in policy decisions (Marks, 2010; Saich,

2010). As a result, each level of government has its own set of concerns. Sometimes these match and sometimes they do not. The disconnect between the central and local governments means that policy outcomes are shaped by the incorporation of the interests of those responsible for implementation. Thus, change is incremental and comes about only through a process of bureaucratic consensus building, or in the words of one, a 'bargaining treadmill' (Lampton, 1987).

One of our interviewees commented on this 'treadmill' and the process of policy formation where consensus is valued above majority rule. Yan Qi, a professor at Tsinghua University, helps draft commissioned reports from various government institutions. When asked what the impact of his work was, Yan answered:

> It is very difficult to locate any specific policy contribution from a particular piece of research in China. Because China's policy making is different from the West in the sense that regulations are products of consensus. Thus all research is to facilitate constructing a consensus within the circle of decision makers, rather than to contribute directly to a specific regulatory act.

Within China's system, broad national strategies are set by those at the top of Party in the Politburo and State Council, while actual legislation and the setting of targets is open to bargaining between bureaucratic agencies. However, at the level of implementation intense bargaining occurs all the way down to local levels of government. At each level, the more powerful regional or bureaucratic units distort policies in directions that are most favourable to them. This results in the process becoming protracted and sometimes severely distorted by the time it has reached the bottom (Mertha, 2009).

Fragmented authoritarianism helps explain why the implementation of environmental and climate policies is fraught with difficulty. Having limited means to coerce regions into acceptance, the central government must make tradeoffs that weaken implementation. Moreover, since power is often vested in certain individuals rather than institutions, citizens and subordinates often have to win the approval of decision makers through giving personal favours rather than by following institutionalised regulations, creating an environment where no single body holds total authority (Marks, 2010).

Under the State Council, China's highest administrative body, there are a number of major institutions implementing China's environmental, energy and climate laws and policies. These include the National Development and Reform Commission (NDRC), which has overall responsibility for China's economic and social development, including climate-change-related policies; the National Energy Commission (NEC); and the MEP. There are also regional and local environmental protection bureaus (EPBs), which are part of the provincial government while concurrently being hierarchically subordinate to the MEP. This dual and complex relationship is vital to understanding the formulation and implementation of laws and policies across all fields in China (Saich, 2010; Tsang and Kolk, 2010).

One key problem of a fragmented system is that governmental units with the same rank cannot issue binding orders to each other (J. Y. Zhang, 2011). This is a problem as central government ministries hold the same status of authority as do provincial governments. This is known as the *tiao–kuai* problem as bureaucratic agencies are interconnected both vertically (*tiao*) and horizontally (*kuai*). In other words, units have to report both to an upper-level department of the same function and the government of a geographical area (Ma and Ortolano, 2000). So a body such as the MEP, while technically part of the State Council, cannot issue a binding order to local government. To complicate matters further, localities often receive investment from industries which EPBs are charged with regulating, so environmental officials are answerable not only to their own ministries but to local Party and government officials who sometimes have a stake in ensuring a particular factory or mine is not hit with crippling environmental action (Economy, 2004; Shapiro, 2012). For example, a provincial level EPB supervises the work of EPBs of counties and districts within the province and reports to the central MEP. Yet the EPB is also part of the provincial government and thus falls under its jurisdiction (Tsang and Kolk, 2010). These two-dimensional arrangements inevitably create conflicts and 'a regular slippage between policy and practice' (McBeath, 2007).

A few of our interviewees commented on how the segregation of administrative remit creates difficulties in bringing about coordinated governance. One example is the regulatory divide between the NDRC and MEP. While climate change falls into the jurisdiction of NDRC, MEP is the authority for air quality control. For Zhu Can, programme officer at CAI-Asia, this creates a gap of knowledge in his work which prevents him from being able to fully compare data with other countries. This is because, as noted in Chapter 3, MEP has been promoting public disclosure of environmental information since May 2008 (State Environmental Protection Administration, 2007). 'To date, statistics on most major air pollutants are made publicly available', said Zhu, 'but data on green house gas and CO_2 are controlled by NDRC and are not in the public domain.'

These issues are made worse by the fact that Beijing delegates the responsibilities of environmental regulatory decisions to local officials, whose policy preferences are crucial (Marks, 2010). Since environmental institutions depend on the local government for financial support, they generally do not oppose the local administration even if that means the continuation of environmental pollution. Furthermore, local administrators are reluctant to implement measures if they are designed to reduce their influence. Since they are often in strong competition with other localities for investment, instead of fully complying with already vague central legislation, local officials often only pay lip service to environmental protection efforts and continue to prioritize economic growth (Shapiro, 2012). We have seen this in many of our examples, where people were concerned about China's environmental problems and thought that protecting the environment was very important in the abstract, but placed a lower priority on environmental protection than on economic and technological development. According to one survey, when provincial officials were asked if they would close a company that was heavily polluting, only a minority said that they would do so (Tong, 2007).

It is not as if China's fragmented system is not a source of alarm for those working within it. For example, China's People's Daily Press publishes a series of books called *Strategies for a Great Nation* (*Daguo Ce*). In 2009, the series published a title on environment protection. A key policy suggestion of the book was to change the segregation of administrative power.

> China has not yet established a routinised coordination system for the implementation of regulations. The most common coordination is to unify relevant administrative institutions under the government for a 'united implementation operation' (*lianhe zhifa xingdong*). Such an approach can often give illegal behaviour a heavy blow and solve law enforcement difficulties, but it is not a long-term solution. Administrative coordination often vanishes once the operation ends.
>
> (Geng, 2009)

From the above, we can see that China's political structure works both for and against environmental causes. Fragmented authoritarianism can inhibit the full effects of a green policy and lead to uneven application. But environmental authoritarianism can rely on 'eco-elites' at the highest level of government to create policies and national targets without the obstacles inherent in a liberal democratic framework.

In Five Years' Time ...

Leading Chinese economist Hu Angang is a clear advocate of environmental authoritarianism. He writes that:

> One of the key strengths of Chinese socialism is its capacity for long-term, national-level planning – its political continuity .... Despite the twists and turns of history, China has held firm in its modernisation goals. China is one of the few nations able to pursue long-term development goals, rather than chop and change as political parties with differing stances succeed one another .... These are strengths many other nations lack.
>
> (Hu and Liang, 2011)

Hu and Liang go on to compare China with the United States, and its changing position on emissions reduction responsibilities under the Kyoto Protocol as power in Washington shifted between the Republicans and Democrats. According to the authors, China has distinct political advantages as only an enduring and stable political system can ensure that a country maintains a consistent, long-term strategy for tackling climate change. This is because such a commitment requires an overhaul of the mode of economic development and individual lifestyles.

Hu and Liang believe China's Five Year Plans (FYPs) are a key component in the country's strategic development. FYPs are blueprints, which provide goals for social and economic growth. They contain previously implemented regional and long-term development plans and hundreds of targeted policy initiatives, all of which undergo constant review and revision over the course of the five-year cycle. The term conjures up memories of old Soviet-style plans but in fact the Chinese term increasingly used to describe the FYP is not *jihua* (plan) but rather *guihua* (programme). This reflects the FYPs' transformation from a straightforward list of economic objectives to a more general guideline for both economic and social policy (APCO, 2010).

The 12th FYP, passed by the National People's Congress in 2011, sets out China's green development strategy to 2015 in considerable detail. The environmental aspects of the plan, which have been much heralded for its ambitious targets, have six overlapping areas: responding to climate change; strengthening conservation and management of resources; developing a 'circular economy'; enhancing environmental protection; promoting ecological protection and restoration; and strengthening systems for water management, and disaster prevention and alleviation. All six of these can be seen in China's attempt to create eco-cities, which we discuss below.

Perhaps the most noteworthy aspect of the 12th FYP is that it deepens a major policy shift away from a focus on 'growth at any cost' toward a more balanced and sustainable growth pattern. The plan aims for average annual GDP growth of 7 per cent – much smaller than the 10 per cent on average achieved over the period of the 11th FYP. This smaller rate reflects the global economic downturn but also illustrates the need to make growth more inclusive. The numbers themselves seem dull but are worth repeating as they show the scale of the government's ambition.

Much of the FYP is devoted to energy, calling for a 16 per cent cut in energy intensity (energy consumed per unit of GDP). The FYP reflects China's pledge to have 15 per cent of its energy come from non-fossil fuels by 2020. To help achieve this, Beijing has set impressive goals for cleaner energy, with substantial changes to its overall mix of fuel supplies. This includes an increase in non-fossil fuel sources of primary energy consumption from 8.3 per cent to 11.4 per cent. As part of its strategy to meet this, the government plans to invest heavily in hydro-electricity and in nuclear power, aiming to build 40 additional gigawatts of nuclear energy capacity by 2015. As one would expect, the FYP also includes massive investment in new wind and solar farms. The natural gas share of the energy mix is slated to grow from 4 per cent to 8 per cent while the plan allows for coal consumption to grow in absolute terms but fall from 70 per cent to 62 per cent of the overall energy mix.

Other targets include:

• A 40–45 per cent cut in carbon intensity and 30 per cent cut in water intensity (the amount of carbon emitted and water consumed per unit of GDP).
• New efforts will be made to implement energy and environmental

taxes as a way of managing limited resources more efficiently, rather than top-down plant closures or other direct orders. Pricing reform will also speed up for the cost of electricity, liquid fuels, water and other resources.

- The FYP aims to boost forests by 600 million cubic metres and forest cover to 21.66 per cent of China.
- Investment in environmental protection is expected to exceed 3 trillion RMB over the five-year period. Much of this will go on pollution control. There is, for example an 8 per cent reduction target for sulphur dioxide demand and a 10 per cent reduction target for ammonia nitrogen and nitrogen oxides, the latter of which comes mainly from coal.
- The plan mandates significant investment in public transportation, including the construction of 35,000 km of high-speed rail and efforts to connect every city with more than 500,000 residents.

Of course, as suggested in the previous section, targets and results are not necessarily the same thing in Chinese politics. The 11th FYP (2006–10) also had considerable environmental goals. These met with mixed results. During the plan period the country's target annual GDP growth rate was routinely exceeded, while in late 2010 local authorities were caught in a last-minute race to meet their energy reduction targets. This rush included temporarily shutting factories and cutting electricity supplies in several cities. In Anping County, in Hebei, for example, the government cut electricity to homes, factories and public buildings for 22 hours every three days (Watts, 2010). In the end, the national target was narrowly missed by 1 per cent (China Greentech Initiative, 2012), and the central government was forced into making a rare public apology for the brownouts and blackouts.

This example shows well the inherent tension between provincial and national goals. Central government targets for GDP growth, energy and the environment conflict in some cases with higher growth targets set at the provincial level than those implied from overall national growth rates. As in the past, the central government will often allow the provinces to decide how to reconcile competing objectives, sometimes leading to uneven enforcement of energy and environmental goals (China Greentech Initiative, 2011).

The FYP and the goals of creating a circular economy, discussed in the next section, hint at significant changes in the meaning of development itself, and implicitly the way China seeks to measure growth and the values associated with it. Around the time of the FYP's release, Zhou Shengxian, Minister of Environmental Protection, made the rather blunt assessment: 'Natural resources are shrinking, degenerating and drying up. Ecological and environmental decay has become a bottleneck and a serious obstacle to our economic and social development. If our homeland is destroyed and we lose our health, then what good does development do?' (Hook, 2011).

Perhaps this is mere rhetoric. We might draw both alarm and solace from the fact that Zhou is also an accomplished economist. Yet there does seem to be a growing discourse against assigning higher priority to economic development than to environmental issues, as the government seeks to internalise environmental objectives as part of the performance evaluation of political leaders. We now turn to two of the more interesting and interrelated ways it is seeking to do this, both of which are featured in the FYP: the notion of a circular economy and the development of eco-cities.

What Goes Around Comes Around

Canadian singer Jack Johnson's pop hit 'The 3 Rs' encourages children to 'reduce, reuse, recycle'. It could easily be the theme song for China's eco-technocrats.

Inspired by Japanese and German recycling laws, Beijing has embraced the idea of a circular economy. This refers to a holistic approach in using resources, prizing efficiency and integrated production in a broader system encompassing networks of industrial firms, eco-industrial parks, and regional infrastructure to support resource optimisation. A circular economy operates by:

- reducing consumption of resources and emission of pollutants and waste
- reusing and recycling resources within industrial parks and industries, so that resources will circulate fully in the local production system
- integrating different production and consumption systems in a region so the resources circulate among industries and urban systems (Preston, 2012).

At present, given the levels of poverty within China, the government's main focus is on meeting people's basic needs while achieving the maximum efficiency of resource use. The government's hope, beyond the benefits to sustainable development discussed below, is that new systems of resource recovery and cleaner production will reap economic rewards through investment in joint ventures and job creation. However, the obstacles to realising a circular economy are immense.

Climatologist Ge Quan reminded us of this:

> I once attended a lecture given by a former climate change advisor to Tony Blair in Beijing. The gist of his talk was that the UK has realized carbon reduction on basis of economic growth, thus China should also follow such path. It was obvious that this British advisor has only been to major cities, such as Guangzhou and Beijing, and didn't know China. His main suggestion was the adoption of hybrid electric cars in the rural areas. So I wrote to him afterwards, asking, 'Sir, with all due respect, can you imagine a Chinese peasant wearing a straw hat and a pair of patched pants driving your hybrid car on a muddy road in rural China?' He later replied and admitted that infrastructure construction is a prerequisite. The difference between China and Europe is that Europe has an existing infrastructure, while large parts of China are still a big construction site.

The challenges of building a circular economy certainly include regional disparities and lack of infrastructure. Beyond this, even though state-owned firms, private enterprises and consumers all have a role in achieving a circular economy, the concept remains a top-down initiative, so the ambitions and expectations of the central government are often not matched by the knowledge and experience of local officials and citizens. Guidelines are either weak or lacking, leaving many local planners unclear how a circular economy differs from standard environmental protection planning. Perhaps more fundamental is the challenge involved in changing consumption patterns to avoid waste, and the tendency, as rife in China as anywhere, simply to throw things away.

A successful circular economy aims to integrate the flow of resources between urban and rural systems. However, given the pace of urbanisation in China, Beijing's attempt to promote these ideas through the development of eco-cities has attracted the most attention. Indeed, eco-cities are a crucial part of a circular economy concept given the scale of urban migration within China, itself an environmental issue.

When Deng launched China's reform era in 1979, it spawned an immense social and ecological shift on a scale and at a rate never before witnessed in human history. In 1980 China was still overwhelmingly rural and agricultural, with just under 200 million people, or 20 per cent of the population, living in cities. By 2013, over 700 million people, or 52 per cent of the population, lived in urban settings. To put this in perspective, since 1980 China's cities have grown by more than the total population of the European Union, which stands at 503 million. It is a trend that will continue. The United Nations forecasts that China's urbanisation rate will reach 60 per cent by 2025 and nearly 80 per cent by 2050. The annual population increase in China's cities over the next 20 years is forecast to be about over 17 million – the equivalent of adding one global megacity, such as New York City, each year (United Nations, 2012).

One key reason for this trend is the strong economic motivation that encourages urbanisation Approximately 167 million people in China's cities are migrant workers who have left the countryside in search of higher wages. The economic output of workers rises dramatically in urban areas, as the value added per agricultural worker in China today is less than a tenth that of a non-agricultural worker, meaning that the more urbanisation continues, the faster China's economy will grow (World Bank, 2009b).

Urbanisation at this scale requires a vast outlay of natural resources to construct new cities, which often replace productive arable land. The higher income level of urban dwellers also leads to greater consumption, as illustrated by the usual status symbols of automobiles, designer goods, expensive homes and so forth. These challenges impact on all major areas: water pollution, waste management, air pollution, energy demand and land utilization, including the conversion of agricultural land to urban use. No wonder then that one of China's leading gardening experts calls the current form of urbanisation a 'path to death' (Watts, 2010: 284).

The government is acutely aware of the challenges of urbanisation and its effect on the environment. So it is no surprise then that China is the world's leader in promoting the concept of eco-cities. The specifics of eco-cities depend on their locality. What they all have in common are radical plans for sustainable development. No detail has been left unplanned. Many eco-cities stipulate that every building must be double-glazed. In some settings, affordable housing, education and medical care are all clustered in the city centre to encourage a thriving civic life. In these green heavens, an electric shuttle service would pass every home and communities would be zoned so people could walk to school, shops and clinics.

Half the road space will be reserved for non-motorised traffic and all homes will be within a two-minute walk of a public park. Technology features heavily in all eco-city plans. Water usage will be cut by relying on new methods of water treatment to make supplies potable and using new rain capture techniques. As implied by the concept of circular economies, eco-cities include ambitious plans to rely on clean and renewable energy and the reuse and recycling of resources (Hald, 2009; Watts, 2010).

The development of eco-cities relies on a mix of public and private funds. One of the most high-profile sites is in Tianjin, just an hour northwest of Beijing. This project is a joint venture between the Chinese government, the Tianjin government and Singapore. It has been supported with funds from the World Bank. The aim is to have a city of 350,000 people by 2020. After government planners had done much of the planning, they sold off plots of land in the city area to individual developers. The Tianjin eco-city is envisioned as an 'economically sustainable, socially harmonious, environmentally friendly and resource-conserving' city (World Bank, 2009b).

Eco-cities are not without considerable problems. Dongtan, for example, was an early showcase which never materialised. Located near Shanghai, this eco-city was announced with great fanfare in 2005 but ran into numerous obstacles. Critics complained that the project was too ambitious and divorced from reality. It was beset with construction delays and design problems, and foreign investors who did not understand the local context. Nor did it help matters when the political leaders who championed the project were arrested for corruption. A key lesson from Dongtan was the need to earn strong support from local governments and local communities to ensure that plans are translated into real development (World Bank, 2009b).

Eco-cities are clearly a work in progress. At present not a single one has been completed. Perhaps they and circular economies will go the way of Beijing's plan to implement a 'Green GDP' – an index of economic growth that factors in the costs of the environmental degradation. First announced in 2004, the government's hopes of implementing the measure were dealt a setback because of problems in actually measuring the cost and opposition from local governments which feared their rates would plummet if the environmental effects were taken into account. Apparently they had some reason to be concerned, as a World Bank report found the total costs of China's air and water pollution to be 5.8 per cent of GDP in 2007 (World Bank and SEPA, 2007).

Whatever the fate of circular economies and eco-cities, both are part of something more fundamental – and, if possible, more ambitious.

An Eco-Soft Power?

Increasingly, the rhetoric of Chinese officials reflects the government's green agenda. Increasingly, it is also tied to a much larger sociopolitical platform. Take for instance, the comments made by a leading environmental official, Pan Yue, in 2004:

> China can no longer afford to follow the West's resources-hungry model of development and it should encourage its citizens to avoid adopting the developed world's consumer habits .... It's important to make Chinese people not blatantly imitate Western consumer habits so as not to repeat the mistakes by the industrial development of the west over the past 300 years.
>
> (Whittington, 2004)

His comments were echoed by former Chinese President Hu Jintao in 2012 at the 18th National Party Congress. In a report prepared for the Congress, the President indicated his belief that:

> The proper path for China's sustainable growth in the future is with ecological progress at its core .... The Industrial Revolution contributed to the prosperity of some Western countries, but at the expense of the environment. These countries paid huge prices later in rehabilitating the environment. The process had been duplicated in some parts of China over the past decades. Aware of the severity of the problem during the process, China is resolved to abandon the same old path that goes from environmental deterioration to rehabilitation, and it now advocates ecological progress to save energy, protect the environment and develop its economy at the same time.
>
> (Hu, 2012)

To the surprise of some, Hu devoted an entire section of his speech to Congress to 'ecological civilisation'. This was a term he first coined in his address to the 17th Party Congress in 2007 to describe his vision of growth and conservation. However, at that time Hu devoted a mere paragraph to the idea, whereas at the 18th Congress it was given the same status as economic, political, cultural and social development.

The concept of an ecological civilisation serves a dual purpose for the Chinese leadership. Importantly, it allows the Party to maintain a discourse – albeit a modified one – of economic growth and prosperity, around which it has built its legitimacy to rule. Beijing maintains an ambitious development target to raise the majority of China's population into 'an all-round well-off society'. In Chinese, the phrase for this idea is a Xiaokang society in which most people are moderately well off and middle class, and in which economic prosperity is sufficient to move most of the population in mainland China into comfortable means, but in which economic advancement is not the sole focus of society. Explicitly incorporated into the concept of a Xiaokang society is the idea that economic growth needs to be balanced with sometimes conflicting goals of social equality and environmental protection.

Beijing hopes that by 2050, when its population will be approximately 1.8 billion, most of its people will reach a per capita GDP of US$4,000 per year, five times the current level. This demands a tremendous increase in production and multiplies pressure on natural resources and the environment. Research by the State Environmental Protection Administration indicates that China's economy will need to achieve at least a sevenfold increase in efficiency of resource use to achieve the goals set for 2050, while maintaining environmental quality (Lei and Qian, 2004).

It is clear that such a goal is not possible given current models of development, as the resources are not available to provide a growing population with higher standards in a high-consumption Western-style lifestyle. The challenge for the Chinese government and people is to create an alternative to Western economic development models. Notions of circular economies, eco-cities and ecological civilisations all fit into this agenda.

Referring to the idea of an ecological civilisation, the *China Daily* in 2007 claimed:

This concept reflects an important change in the Party's under-standing of development. Rather than emphasising economic construction as the core of development as it did in the past, the Party authorities have come to realise that development, if sustain-able, must entail a list of elements including the right relationship between man and nature. This concept is proposed at a time when 62 per cent of the country's major rivers have been seriously polluted, 90 per cent of waterways flowing through urban areas are contaminated, more than 300 million residents are yet to have clean water to drink, and quite a number of localities fail to fulfil the required quotas for pollutant emission reduction and energy saving. Facing such a reality, the construction of ecological civilisation was absolutely not rhetoric for chest thumping by officials in their speeches. It needs to be transformed into tangible measures that will change the way our economy develops.

(China Daily, 2007)

The editorial goes on to assert that the concept of an ecological civilisation contains a much broader meaning then mere environmental protection. It also holds important insights into the cultural dimension of development – into both the need to consider nature as part of life rather than something to be exploited without restraint, and the need to maintain a sense of fairness so disadvantaged social groups also realise their right to development.

It is here that we see the second broad purpose the ecological civilisation discourse serves for the government: it serves as a soft power tool to help promote China's image as an alternative to the West, an alternative that places greater emphasis not only on long-term sustainability but also on the need for inclusive growth (Barr, 2012). That China currently has a widening income gap should not be taken as evidence to contradict this. It is, rather, evidence that the Party has a keen sense that it needs to address issues of justice – ecological and social – or else it will perish. Hu Jintao said as much at the 18th Party Congress when he expressed his concern that social disparities could be the death knell of the Party-state.

A number of our interviews highlighted the soft power and image-related aspects of promoting green initiatives. Yan Yingquan, a policy analyst based at the Climate Policy Initiative at Tsinghua University, often received work on commission from local governments seeking advice on low-carbon city planning. At the time we met her in a cafeteria in Tsinghua, Yan had just concluded two such projects. One was for a northern industrial provincial capital and the other was for a small southern village town near Macau. Yan felt both of her clients had additional motives for seeking her professional advice. She told us:

They both took the initiative to come all the way to Beijing and ask us to tailor a low-carbon plan for their city. They have the money for such investments and clearly thought it's quite a trendy thing to pursue. They feel to spend their money on building low-carbon cities is to add some credit to their political achievement. They are very small cities, and this [low-carbon] will be like one of their brands to help to establish their names.

Yan's views were supported by another interviewee, Wang Lan, a project manager at a British consulting company in Beijing specialising in setting up CDM projects in China. She praised China's strong support for CDM but felt that a strong sense of 'image-building' was a key factor.

China is perhaps one of the best at encouraging CDM projects. Whenever we help our client develop CDM applications, we need to ask the local Development and Reform Commission for assistance. In almost every case, the local Commission has been very collaborative. I felt that this [general level of support] was not related to any immediate interests, but was seen as connected to local image-building. For example, in one of the cases, the head of the local Environmental Protection Bureau actually followed the progress closely in person. He kept on checking with the local enterprises and our client hurried us to finish it. I felt that must be because the CDM project was counted as a local political achievement and related to the local image.

Even though the notion of an ecological civilisation represents more of a future hope than a description of the present, it should not be dismissed too readily. While the Xi Jinping government may emphasise different aspects of the principle, it is unlikely it will stray far from the core idea. Even before formally taking office, Chinese Premier Li Keqiang gave a speech reaffirming the commitment to an ecological civilisation, adding that if China could find the right balance between sustainability and development, it would be 'a big contribution to the whole of mankind' (Li, 2012). This is because there is no escape from the fact that China has paid an extremely high price for its for economic miracles, both environmentally and socially. An ecological civilisation allows the Party to recoup some of these losses by sustaining both growth and its own right to rule.

The Politics of Harmony

The idea of an ecological civilization is itself part of Hu Jintao's 'scientific development concept'. This refers to the need to take

Chinese people's interests as the 'starting point and foothold' of all policy. The concept is an amorphous one, which has been criticised for its lack of substantive content. In China's constitution, it is defined as a principle that 'puts people first and calls for comprehensive, balanced and sustainable development'. According to China expert Joseph Fewsmith, the idea 'aims to correct the presumed overemphasis in recent years on the pursuit of increases in gross domestic product, which encourages the generation of false figures and dubious construction projects along with neglect for the social welfare of those left behind in the hinterland' (Fewsmith, 2004).

A central plank of the concept is Hu's call for a 'harmonious society' (hexie shehui), and its foreign policy counterpart, a 'harmonious world' (hexie shijie). The two programmes are intertwined, and are both directly related to green politics, for their goals include the amelioration of social divisions brought about by environmental problems, including widening regional disparities, endemic corruption, a poor social and welfare system, massive unemployment and structural poverty. The concepts seek to address these problems both within China and across the North/South divide. Combined, these issues have badly affected the Party's image. Unlike his predecessors who developed rather pragmatic theories of socialism with Chinese characteristics, Hu was thus compelled to look into issues beyond economic development, and as a result, over his time in power, he developed the tenure socio-economic vision described in this chapter (Zheng and Sow, 2007).

Of particular interest here is the notion of a harmonious world, which reaffirms and extends the idea of peaceful development – the idea that unlike previous great powers, China's rise would not be accompanied by violent transitions in the international system. In practice, the harmonious world doctrine has seen China play a more proactive role in international relations, especially on issues associated with global poverty. Importantly, the doctrine maintains that Beijing's foreign policy is an extension of its domestic policy. Thus, in environmental affairs, if a harmonious society promotes green growth and a more equitable society, a harmonious world advocates fair and just international environmental rules according to the principle of 'common but differentiated responsibility' laid out by the Kyoto Protocol.

This is evident from China's negotiating tactics at COP15 in 2009 in Copenhagen. It was harshly criticised in the West, most notably by then UK climate secretary Ed Miliband, for wrecking a global climate deal. A leaked Chinese government memo, however, gave

Beijing's account of the talks. Chinese officials were rather proud that at COP15 they had managed to resist a deal proposed by rich nations which would have put an unacceptable burden on China and other developing countries. As reported by the *Guardian* in the UK, an internal Chinese government document:

> argued that 'the overall interests of developing countries have been defended' by resisting a rich nation 'conspiracy' to abandon the Kyoto Protocol, and with it the legal distinction between rich nations that must cut carbon emissions and developing nations for whom action is not compulsory.
>
> (Watts, Carrington and Goldenberg, 2010)

This line fits neatly, of course, with China's claims that developing nations with no historical responsibility for carbon emissions cannot be held to the same standards as industrialised countries.

The principle of common but differentiated responsibility has domestic relevance too. Chen Qi, the engineer from Shenzhen we visited in the Introduction, explained to us:

> Similar to the Yangtze delta, the Pearl River delta also consists of three rivers: the East, North and West River. The North River used to provide drinking water to Guangzhou. But during last year's fieldwork I saw it was already polluted by factories. So currently Guangzhou has turned to the West River for drinking water. But this won't be a quality water source for long, because upstream communities have also decided to seek higher GDP. You can't blame them. Since we all drink from the same river, when people living upstream see that regions of the delta are well developed, of course they seek the same. But they don't have the technological, financial or labour support. The quickest way to get rich is to take advantage of your natural resources. But this has severe environment impact .... You can't deny people's right to development. The compromise would be for regions in the delta to set up a financial support system to upstream regions, so that they won't exploit their natural resources and we can save a valuable source of drinking water. But this idea is hard to operate in practice. Working between provinces is difficult. It requires central government's mediation.

Chen reminds us that actors within China at different levels hold common duties. This is perhaps what we would expect. Yet coming to a 'harmonious' resolution about these obligations is no easy task. It is understandable then that people are sceptical about the politics of harmony, and for that matter about the chances of China building an ecological civilisation. There is some similarity between these grand designs and Mao's ideological campaigns. Both hold utopian ideals, fuelled by science and progress; both stem from the top down but require mass mobilization if they are to succeed. But as many point out, it is hypocritical to call for a harmonious society that 'puts people first' when you simultaneously block people's access to information which affects them and lock up those who publicly question your authority. Similarly, it does not help Beijing's image to be calling for an ecological civilisation when the government is refusing to release data on the quality of the air its people must breathe.

The green leap forward described in this chapter – FYPs, circular economies, eco-cities and civilizations – shows that the government has a clear vision of the future. It is one dominated by green tech in pursuit of sustainability. But more importantly, these approaches reflect the reality of China's situation and needs as they currently exist. It is impossible for China to achieve its development by following the same path as the West has over the last few hundred years. The challenge for the government is how to convince its people that bigger is not better and having more is not patriotic.

CONCLUSION:
TO STOMACH A GREEN SOCIETY

China's Central Television, known for its dry political content and propaganda-driven agendas, surprisingly captivated the Chinese community around the globe with a seven-episode documentary, *A Bite of China*. Focused on Chinese gastronomy, the series not only became the most popular show in China, but also made many overseas Chinese homesick for their favourite dishes (Z. Y. Wu, 2012; L. Zhang, 2012). Employing first-class cinematography, *A Bite of China* incorporated different types of cuisine and snacks from 60 different locations around the country. However, the huge success of this series lay in the fact that it was not limited to the preparation and making of the food itself. It also explored the cultural history behind the food as well as the personal stories of chefs and street vendors. In short, it gave a human touch to Chinese food.

First shown in May 2012, *A Bite of China* was seen as the latest addition to China's soft power by the international community. Made available in English, French, Portuguese and Spanish, it won numerous plaudits at the 65th Annual Cannes Film Festival (Chen, 2012). Domestically, the reception of the show was twofold. On the one hand, it enjoyed huge popularity. Through a narrative of rediscovering the arts and histories of Chinese cooking, it indulged the audience with a wealth of heritage of Chinese civilisation. On the other hand, as the viewers subsequently set out to look for the food that had been so deliciously presented on the show, or at least the ingredients with which to make the dishes, a stark reality hit people: the reality of food safety in China. Commentators made sarcastic remarks that for ordinary Chinese, their everyday meal was not so much 'a bite of China', but rather 'a bite of the periodic table' (L. Zhang, 2012).

As we discussed in Chapter 3, illegal industrial waste has brought about severe water and soil pollution. Plants grown in such environments have a heavy metal content that has had serious health effects (J. Liu, 2012). The MEP was compelled to devote 30 billion RMB on soil remediation in its 12th FYP, in part because of food safety fears (Yan, 2012). In addition, as a result of poor law enforcement in food processing and quality control, many products on the market do not meet health safety standards. This can be seen from the changing vocabularies in Chinese kitchens. For example 'gutter oil' (*digouyou*), refers to illicit cooking oil produced by recycling waste from drains and slaughter houses. 'Leather milk' (*pigenai*) refers to leather scraps being mixed into raw milk supplies to boost protein-test results. The domestic reception of *A Bite of China* is perhaps a good demonstration of the contrast and the subsequent sting felt by ordinary Chinese when an 'ecological civilisation' meets ecological reality. This is especially true for a country whose 2,000 years of political philosophy were underwritten by the recognition that 'food is the paramount necessity of people'.

Being denied a safe dining table is perhaps the most powerful warning sign to Chinese on what has gone wrong. Ruthless natural exploitation, short-sighted development plans, incompetent bureaucracy, weak public oversight, dilapidated social trust and yet large parts of a society still impatient for wealth – these are just a few samples of the issues that perplex China today.

This book started its empirical examination of China's green politics from the increasingly compelling question of 'who is to blame?', or who should be held accountable for China's degrading environment. This is a question to which Chinese society is still seeking, comparing and debating answers. However, on the basis of the evidence demonstrated, it is safe to conclude that to have a green society, 'China' needs to stomach serious changes. By China, we mean not only commitments from the government, and a more organised and empowered civil society, but also serious thought about the means and ends in pursuing a good life at the individual level.

From Mass Unconsciousness to Citizen Stakeholders

'The price Chinese society is paying for a degrading environment is caused by a 'mass unconsciousness' (*jiti wu yishi*)', Fan Xiaoxi, a Shanghai environmental volunteer, told us. For Fan, and many other activists we interviewed, environmental deterioration was not simply a fault with law enforcement or the consequences of China's rise. It was also the result of more embedded social norms and behaviours that society had to face up to and take responsibility for. 'You can't make changes when only a minority of environmentalists realize where the problem lies', Fan went on to say. 'You need to make the majority share the same view. This is difficult, but we must confront this problem head on.'

Seen from the perspective of the many ENGO initiatives discussed in this book, the type of 'mass unconsciousness' described by Fan Xiaoxi can be summarised in two ways. The first is a general lack of knowledge of the connection between personal lifestyle and its environmental impact. In some cases, we realise this point is open to debate, for consumers might well know that their acts have environmental consequences and yet choose to proceed all the same. Nonetheless, according to the experience of Fan and others we have encountered, it is also the case that some people simply are not aware of the effects of their behaviour. The second point relating to this is a lack of consciousness of their rights amongst the Chinese public.

As discussed in Chapters 2 and 5, the general failure of people to make the link between their personal lifestyle and its environmental consequences is partly a result of progressive urbanisation and a common aspiration to embrace modern (that is, Western-style) lifestyles. In some cases, this may also lead to situations where consumption habits effectively encourage the compromise of green commitments. For example, in recent years, golf has become an increasingly popular sport in China, for it has the aura of an upper-class Western sport. In some cases, golf was also seen by Chinese 'tiger moms' as a skill that could to help their children's future application to American universities (Li, 2012). But the construction of golf courses can also be 'extremely deleterious to the surrounding environment: the clearing of natural vegetation, deforestation, destruction of natural landscapes and habitats and changes in local topography and hydrology' are all possible hazards (Wheeler and Nauright, 2006: 431). In addition, building golf courses aggravates China's land resource shortage. Thus, in 2004, the Chinese central government banned the construction of golf courses. However, many local governments have sanctioned the construction of golf courses nonetheless as they drive up local housing prices and promote the local economy. In the eight years from 2004 to 2012, despite the ban, China built 400 new golf courses (Ci, 2012; Fang, 2012). This raises the prospect of an interesting paradox: are those who go to illicit golf clubs (or for that matter, consume products from companies guilty of illegal dumping) also the people who complain about degraded air quality, contaminated water and a shrinking choice of safe vegetables?

It was this 'mass unconsciousness' of the many causal relations embedded in consumption patterns that incentivised Chinese ENGOs to organise public engagement and education programmes, to which Fan Xiaoxi has been a regular contributor. 'I know I can only influence a small circle of people,' Fan said, 'but even this small influence at the grassroots is needed.'

Similarly, Huo Jian, who was a long-term volunteer for a couple of grassroots ENGOs, explained the importance of working with the masses in China through the analogy of a pyramid:

> You need to have a pyramid structure in pushing this [environmental protection] forward. Normally everyone wants to be at the tip of the pyramid, but in the case of China, there is a hollow bottom and everything is vulnerable to collapse. Thus it is true that grassroots NGOs may not have a strong voice, but I still support them because I think they are exactly what's needed in China: to create a large and solid mass foundation that can hold up all the passionate ideas.

Interactions with the public were not limited to just letting more people know of the connection between environmental cost and developmental values. The recognition of causal relations may also prompt a collective desire for action. As one staff at the ENGO Green Stone said, 'quantitative change can lead to qualitative change':

> It is most important for Chinese ENGOs to share their information and experience with the public. Because these experiences send out a signal and make the public see that things can be changed. They can also take action.

Here we see the second point which follows on from the notion of mass unconsciousness. Wang Wei, whose work included leading weekend workshops on domestic waste assortment in different neighbourhoods, saw her work as 'promoting a basic idea' of citizen rights:

> What I am doing in building the blocks may only bring behavioural change in a limited number of people .... But people like me working for ENGOs collectively send out a message to the wider public and help them to recognise that there are many little things in everyday life that concern individual rights. We hope the public

can recognise what their rights are, and how to take action to honour those rights. We are promoting a basic idea: When you see what should be done, then it is within your legal rights to pursue or demand it.

Thus a main objective, and in some cases the major contribution, of China's grassroots activism is to turn the 'unconscious' mass into 'citizen stakeholders'. Grassroots activism qualifies as a mass (re)education of citizenship, because through various online and offline campaigns, ENGOs not only remind ordinary Chinese of their legal rights and the duties associated with their membership of a political community. More importantly, through events such as public environmental monitoring and taking advantage of the Open Information Act, ENGOs have demonstrated to the public how to defend and exercise their rights. Bottom-up green initiatives also serve as a channel to turn indifferent members of the public into 'stakeholders'. Photographic lessons, bird-watching and outdoor 'natural experience' events are not simply one way of disseminating environment knowledge. They also invite participants' self-reflections on how they situate themselves within the natural and social milieu of contemporary China. Such events help the public to recognise that they have a direct stake in the social and political decisions regarding China's path to modernisation.

At the end of China's 11th National People's Congress (NPC) in 2012, the Standing Committee of the NPC held a special session on the environment. The official statistics show that serious environmental accidents increased by a stunning 120 per cent in 2011. But at the same time, the frequency of ENGO events in China also exhibited a 29 per cent annual increase since 1996 (Shu Wang, 2012). With more Chinese starting to see themselves as 'citizen stakeholders', China may be a step closer to a green society.

Speak Truth to Power

The phrase 'speak truth to power' was coined by the American Friends Service Committee (AFSC) in one of its studies on the peaceful solution to the rise of fascism in the 20th century. This original publication drew out three connotations of the word 'power'. It refers to those who bear the responsibility of making critical decisions; the people who grant legitimacy to the established authorities; and the idea of power itself (AFSC, 1955: iv).

The Chinese version of 'speak truth to power' (*xiang quanli sushuo zhenli*) was popularised by ecologist Jiang Gaoming, who was among 36 leading scholars invited to contribute to the book *Journey of the Souls*, published in 2006 as a collective review of changes in China in the 30 years since the Cultural Revolution. Jiang encapsulated his career journey in China's environmental protection sector with the phrase 'speak truth to power' (Jiang, 2006).

To the general public, Jiang was known for helping damaged ecosystems to recover naturally. This idea first came from his work on controlling sandstorms in Beijing. Through his experiments from 2000 to 2002 in inner Mongolia, Jiang found the planting of grass rather than trees could reduce the risk of sandstorms. Jiang challenged the effectiveness of the government's proposed 73-year agenda, the Three-North Shelter Forest Programme, established in 1978. Unsurprisingly, he earned the label of an 'unpopular person' with government authorities (Jiang, 2006).

Jiang's approach of using empirical evidence and scientific thinking in critically examining environmental policies resembles a basic rationale shared by most of the homegrown ENGOs we interviewed. While the observation that China's civil environmental groups 'lack the capability of conducting empirical studies and setting up professional dialogues' and 'availing [themselves of] legal channels in seeking effective (environmental) protections' (Feng, 2009: 185) may have been true a few years ago, in our research, ENGOs were increasingly astute in data collection and in formulating evidence-based arguments. This was not only true in various civic monitoring activities, but also in pressuring companies to be accountable, in making policy proposals, and in gaining transnational support. Gao Teng, who works at Green Stone, emphasised the importance of data:

> NGOs should remain neutral. We share our research results and the information we have with the public. Our biggest contribution in making social change is to help clarify the facts and details. A public display of facts alone can sometimes help to make progress on things.

To 'get the facts straight' forms the backbone of many of ENGO campaigns. Similarly, working to get the regulations right also provides an effective tool for bottom-up initiatives. As discussed in Chapters 3 and 4, for homegrown ENGOs, finding practical solutions to environmental crises is paramount, but reinforcing the rule of law is no less important. This is a result of both operational considerations and an ambition to initiate long-term, large-scale progress on green issues. On the first point, Mu Shuihe, director of an ENGO in Beijing told us:

> You need to know how society operates, the weakness of the institutions, the structure of the laws, the interests of the media, and the real fears of enterprises, that's how you can make your 'point' in fighting pollution, a point others can't easily ignore .... You have to be aware of all these things, if you want to intervene in society, or rather, truly be part of it.

To be sure, having rules and complying with them are the prerequisites of being a 'civil' society.

As demonstrated in Chapters 2 and 3, the type of power Chinese ENGOs scrutinise is not just political, but also includes the power of business giants that hold economic leverage. The agent that carries out oversight of power holders and demands that they respond could be an individual, a group or the general public.

The trajectory of Chinese development over the 30 years from 1980 can be seen as a continuous returning of rights from the state to society. With the opening-up policy, the Chinese people regained the rights of development and investment. The 2007 Property Law officially restored private property rights. The 2008 Disclosure of Government Information Act recognised the public's right to know. Grassroots environmental activism has also struggled for basic political rights, such as the right to know, the right to a public hearing, and the right to civil disobedience. To some extent, these bottom-up initiatives have already yielded significant results. For ENGOs have not only survived but in some cases, thrived – growing through all the public campaigns to push the political boundaries in state–society relations beyond what was possible a decade ago.

Similar to the AFSC's original scope of speaking truth to power, there also seem to be three dimensions of power with which ENGOs are in conversation: the dissemination of ideas, the deployment of empirical evidence, and the creative search for alternative solutions. All three have served to empower the general public and restrain government authority. In the process, ENGOs have challenged and transformed what constitutes and legitimates a 'power' in Chinese society.

Puzzled but Determined

In many ways the Chinese government has always been confident in pushing forward its agenda. It helps, perhaps, that its people are often willing to conform. It also helps that the leadership has usually known what Chinese society wants and needs. It has not always been given these things, but looking back, Beijing has been far more responsive than it is sometimes given credit for. However the political equation used to be straightforward: set the target, deliver, and the secure the Party's legitimacy. It was never quite than simple, of course, but if nothing else, China's leaders have been pragmatic. They has set clear (economic) goals, and then concentrated all the country's resources on realising those goals. When Deng Xiaoping came to power, he offered China the conceptual tools to merge a market economy with Marxist-Leninist thought. After Deng, Jiang Zemin put forth the idea of 'Three Represents', which asserted that the Party had to represent the development trends of advanced productive forces, advanced culture, and the fundamental interests of the Chinese people. In practice, his policy was a clever means to help boost Party membership by allowing the same groups that Mao had so ruthlessly opposed – the managerial and business classes – to join in and prosper.

The results have been dramatic. No other political organisation in history has improved the lives of so many people in such a short space of time as the Chinese Communist Party. How do you lift a half a billion people over the poverty line in a mere 30 years and still manage to – barely, perhaps – hold things together? But sailing into the 21st century, the Chinese government must feel a bit puzzled, betrayed even. Why are urban white collar workers still not satisfied with their lives? Why do people side with the Americans rather than the Party on air quality monitoring? Why does the Chinese government still have to confront Western criticism while its grassroots activists receive international environmental awards? After all, aren't economic rights human rights too, according to the UN Charter?

The frustration could be seen in Xi Jinping's now famous speech in Mexico in 2009, when he lambasted critics by arguing that China had made its contribution to the financial crisis by making sure its own 1.3 billion people were fed. And yet, he said 'there are a few foreigners, with full bellies, who have nothing better to do than try to point fingers at our country .... China does not export revolution, hunger, poverty, nor does it cause you any headaches. Just what else do you want?' (Moore, 2009).

It has dawned on China's leaders that the answer might be this: people want to be able to eat their rice without worrying about it being contaminated with high levels of the heavy metal cadmium

(Gong, 2011). So following Deng's and Jiang's development-oriented doctrines, Hu Jintao devised the notion of a harmonious society, as we saw in Chapter 5. Growth in and of itself was no longer enough.

But now that, in rhetoric at least, the government has turned its attention to maintaining a balance between development and overall well-being, how does it realise this harmonious vision? The answer, it seems, is evident in the very phrase itself: society. Increasingly the government will need to adapt to an expanding civil society – one that plays a greater role in the bargaining processes so typical of Chinese policy making. To be sure, this trend has already begun, as we have documented. We can be equally sure there is a long way to go. The scale and complexity of environmental problems and the need to reach solutions which can be accepted by the population all exceed the grasp of government power. But this does not mean the authorities need to fear China's activists, for their goals are not dissimilar. As we have shown, state and civil society actors have never been monolithic, with fixed interests or modes of action.

Concluding Thoughts

At the time of finishing this book, three events related to our themes took place. The Beijing Municipal Environmental Monitoring Centre (2012) was set to include three new indicators in Beijing's air quality control programme: PM2.5, carbon monoxide and ozone levels. Teng Anyu had just finished a weekend's botanical workshop with a group of Beijing school children, feeling both frustrated and amused that the only 'plant' that had sparked enthusiasm from the audience was the computer game 'Plants versus zombies'. And to the delight of many, *A Bite of China* announced the launch of a second season in 2013.

For most Chinese, everyday life carries on as usual, with some progress and a few new things to look forward to. After public debate on matters such as air quality, extreme weather conditions and food safety, the forthcoming season of *A Bite of China* will perhaps not only lift up the public's appetite, but also serve as food for thought on the values and beliefs which may have been overlooked. To some extent, a society is like a balloon: it can fly high when filled with the right type of air. Or it can pop if the shocks are too severe. The blast of fresh air brought in by ENGOs is inflating the social sphere with civic dynamics that honour the rule of law. Meanwhile, the government is learning to stomach an increasingly pluralised political sphere. To be sure, much work needs to be done. But China seems to have already experienced the first taste of a green society.

REFERENCES

Aldhous, P. (2005) 'China's burning ambition', *Nature*, 435, 1152–4.

American Friends Service Committee (AFSC) (1955) *Speak Truth to Power: A Quaker search for an alternative to violence.* Philadelphia, Pa.: AFSC.

Anderson, B. (1983) *Imagined Communities: Reflections on the origin and spread of nationalism.* London: Verso.

APCO Worldwide (2010) *China's 12th Five-Year Plan: How it actually works and what's in store for the next five years*, December 10. Beijing, Shanghai: APCO Worldwide.

Apple Inc. (2012) *Apple Supplier 2012 Progress Report*, January. Cupertino, Calif.: Apple Inc.

Bai, H. J. (2010) *Carbon Empire: Carbon capitalism and our bible* (in Chinese). Beijing: China Friendship Press.

Barr, M. (2011) *Who's Afraid of China? The challenge of Chinese soft power.* London: Zed.

Barr, M. (2012) 'Nation branding as nation building: China's image campaign', *East Asia*, 29, 81–94.

Barr, M. and Zhang, J. Y. (2010) 'Bioethics and biosecurity education in China', pp. 115–29 in B. Rappert (ed.), *Ethics, Education, and the Life Sciences.* Canberra: Australian National University Press.

Beck, U., Blok, A., Tyfield, D. and Zhang, J. Y. (2013) 'Cosmopolitan communities of climate risk: conceptual and empirical suggestions for a new research agenda', *Global Networks*, 13(1), 1–21.

Beeson, M. (2010) 'The coming of environmental authoritarianism', *Environmental Politics*, 19(2), 276–94.

Beijing Municipal Environmental Monitoring Centre (2012) 'New air quality monitor data release platform to be launched next year', December 28.

Belk, R. W. and Tumbat, G. (2005) 'The cult of Macintosh', *Consumption Markets and Culture*, 8(3), 205–17.

Bell, D. (2012) 'What China can teach Europe', *New York Times*, January 7. </www.nytimes.com/2012/01/08/opinion/sunday/what-china-can-teach-europe.html?_r=2&ref=global-home&> (accessed December 15, 2012).

Biggs, S. (2010) 'Rutgers' Chinese solar panels show clean-energy shift', Bloomberg, July 23. <www.bloomberg.com/news/2010-07-22/rutgers-chinese-connection-signals-solar-panels-coming-to-roof-near-you.html> (accessed December 15, 2012).

Bourdieu, P. (1980[1990]) *The Logic of Practice*. Stanford, Calif.: Stanford University Press.

Boyd, O. and Copsey, T. (2012) 'What's in the Five-Year Plan?' pp. 13–15 in China Dialogue (eds), *China's Green Revolution: Energy, environment and the 12th Five-Year Plan*. Beijing: China Dialogue Report.

Boykoff, M. T. (2011) *Who Speaks for the Climate? Making sense of media reporting on climate change*. Cambridge: Cambridge University Press.

Bradsher, K. (2009) 'China racing ahead of US in the drive to go solar', *New York Times*, August 24. <www.nytimes.com/2009/08/25/business/energy-environment/25solar.html> (accessed December 15, 2012).

Bradsher, K. (2010) 'China leading global race to make clean energy', *New York Times*, January 30. <www.nytimes.com/2010/01/31/business/energy-environment/31renew.html> (accessed December 15, 2012).

Bradsher, K. (2012) 'China asks embassies to stop measuring air pollution', *New York Times*, June 6. <www.nytimes.com/2012/06/06/world/asia/china-asks-embassies-to-stop-measuring-air-pollution.html?_r=0> (accessed December 15, 2012).

Cao, K. and Cheng, Z. L. (2012) 'Commentary: China's ecological progress determines more than its own future', *Xinhua News Press*, November 13. <http://english.peopledaily.com.cn/90785/8015982.html> (accessed December 15, 2012).

Chan, Stephanie (2008) 'Cross-cultural civility in global civil society: transnational cooperation in Chinese NGOs', *Global Networks*, 8(2), 232–52.

Chakrabortty, A (2012) 'Apple: why doesn't it employ more US workers?' *Guardian* (UK), April 23. <www.guardian.co.uk/technology/2012/apr/23/bad-apple-employ-more-us-workers> (accessed December 15, 2012).

Chen, J. (1996) *Chinese Bird Culture* (in Chinese). Shanghai: Academia Press.

Chen, W. (2012) '*A Bite of China* hot in air. Director use food to exhibit the tastes in life,' May 16, Xinwen Chenbao. <http://ent.ifeng.com/tv/news/mainland/detail_2012_05/16/14566030_0.shtml> (accessed December 15, 2012).

Chen, Y. and Wang, J. (2012) 'Beijing Metrological Station: 14 million hits the limit of warning capacity', *The Economic Observer* (in Chinese), July 24. <http://tech.sina.com.cn/t/2012-07-24/16417423123.shtm>l (accessed December 15, 2012).

Chen, Z. X. (2000) 'Special environment envoys appointments made by State Administration of Environmental Protection', *People's Daily*, June 5. <http://rmrbw.net/simple/index.php?t1248837.html> (accessed December 15, 2012).

China Daily (2007) 'Ecological civilization'. <www.chinadaily.com.cn/> (accessed December 15, 2012).

China Greentech Initiative (2011) *The China Greentech Report 2011: China's Emergence as a global greentech market leader*. Hong Kong: GreenTech Networks.

China Greentech Initiative (2012) *The China Green Tech Report 2012: Faced with Challenges, China accelerates greentech growth*. Hong Kong: GreenTech Networks.

China National Radio (CNR) (2012) 'Chen Guangbiao fresh air marketed, projected annual sale exceeds 1 billion', China National Radio. <http://news.sohu.com/20120812/n350461978.shtml> (accessed December 15, 2012).

China News (2011) 'CR Snow intended to promote environment protection, retrieving the whole story of "traversing Kekexili"', *China News*, October 22. <www.chinanews.com/cj/2011/10-22/3406943.shtml> (accessed December 15, 2012).

China News (2012) '465 deaths in all natural disasters occurred in the first half of 2012', *China News*, July 9. <www.chinanews.com/gn/2012/07-09/4019069.shtml> (accessed December 15, 2012).

Ci, X. (2012) 'Local authority ignore central ban, golf courses increased by 400 in 8 years', *China Youth Daily*, August 30. <http://env.people.com.cn/n/2012/0830/c1010-18871975.html> (accessed December 15, 2012).

Cooper, C. M. (2006) "This is our way in': the civil society of environmental NGOs in south-west China', *Government and Opposition*, **41**(1), 109–36.

Delingpole, J. (2010) 'What the Chinese really think of 'man made global warming', *Telegraph* blog, August 11. <http://blogs.telegraph.co.uk/news/jamesdelingpole/100050359/what-the-chinese-really-think-of-man-made-global-warming/> (accessed December 15, 2012).

Deng, H. J. (2012) 'Why there is no "Chinese Apple",' *Guangming Daily*, December 15. <http://politics.gmw.cn/2012-12/15/content_6024533.htm> (accessed December 15, 2012).

DiFrancesco, D. A. and Young, N. (2011) 'Seeing climate change: the visual construction of global warming in Canadian national print media', *Cultural Geographies*, **18**, 517–36.

Dikotter, F. (2010) *Mao's Great Famine: The story of China's most devastating catastrophe*. London: Bloomsbury.

Duan, H. X. (2010) 'The public perspective of carbon capture and storage for CO_2 emission reductions in China', *Energy Polity*, **38**(9), 5281–9.

Duhigg, C. and Greenhouse, S. (2012) 'Electronic giant vowing reforms in China plants', *New York Times*, March 29. <www.nytimes.com/2012/03/30/business/apple-supplier-in-china-pledges-changes-in-working-conditions.html> (accessed December 15, 2012).

Economy, E. (2004) *The River Runs Black: The environmental challenges to China's future*. Ithaca, N.Y.: Cornell University Press.

Economy, E. (2005) 'China's environmental movement', testimony before the Congressional Executive Commission on China Roundtable on Environmental NGOs in China: Encouraging Action and Addressing Public Grievances. Washington DC, February 7. <www.facetofacemedia.ca/files/Elizabeth%20Economy%20Chinas%20environmental%20movement%20CFR.pd> (accessed December 15, 2012).

Economy, E (2006) 'Environmental governance: the emerging economic dimension', *Environmental Politics*, **15**(2), 149–70.

Entman, Robert M. (1993) 'Framing: toward clarification of a fractured paradigm', *Journal of Communication*, **43**(4), 51–8.

Fan, C. C. (2006) 'China's Eleventh Five-Year Plan (2006–2010): from "Getting Rich First" to "Common Prosperity"', *Eurasian Geography and Economics*, **47**(6), 708–23.

Fang, J. P. (2012) 'Villa and golf courses constructions still ongoing, why central government's ban failed', *People's Daily Online*, July 3. <http://house.people.com.cn/n/2012/0703/c164220-18430859.html> (accessed December 15, 2012).

Fei, X.-T. (1948[1992]). *From the Soil*. Berkeley and Los Angeles, Calif.: University of California Press.

Feng, J. and Lv, Z. S. (2011) 'I monitor the air for my country', *Southern Weekend*, October 28. <www.infzm.com/content/64281> (accessed December 15, 2012).

Feng, Y. F. (2008) *A Country without Trees: An environmental sojourn of a eco-defender* (in Chinese). Beijing: Law Press.

Feng, Y. F. (2009) *Environmental Protection with Lies: Internal reference of EP for the public* (in Chinese). Beijing: World Affair Press.

Feng, Y. F. (2010) *Crying for Civil Force of Environmental Protection* (in Chinese). Beijing: Intellectual Property Press.

Feng, Y. F. (2011) *How to Protect the Environment: Chinese folk legend of environmental protection*. Beijing: World Affair Press.

Ferguson, B. and McCarthy, M. (2009) 'Countdown to Copenhagen: the "people's summit"', *Independent* (UK), November 30. <www.independent.co.uk/environment/climate-change/countdown-to-copenhagen-the-peoples-summit-1831098.html> (accessed December 15, 2012).

Fewsmith, J. (2004) 'Promoting the scientific development concept', *China Leadership Monitor*, no, 11.

Friends of Nature (FON), Institute of Public and Environmental Affairs (IPE) and Green Beagle (2011) 'The other side of Apple', January 20. Beijing: FON, IPE and Green Beagle.

FON, IPE, Green Beagle, Envirofriends, Green Stone and Environmental Action Network (2011) 'The other side of Apple II: pollution spreads through Apple's supply chain', August 31. Beijing: FON, IPE and Green Beagle.

Frolic, M. (1997) 'State-led civil society', pp. 46–67 in T. Brook and M. Frolic (eds), *Civil Society in China*. Armonk, N.Y.: M. E. Sharpe.

Gao, M. (2006) 'Two ministries joined in investigating of Baiyangdian's dead fish', *Beijing News* (in Chinese), April 3. <http://news.xinhuanet.com/fortune/2006-04/03/content_4378908_3.htm> (accessed December 15, 2012).

Geng, S. G. (ed.) (2009) *The Environment Protection and Development Strategies for China: The road to become a great nation*. Beijing: People's Daily Press.

Gereffi, G. and Fernandez-Stark, K. (2011) *Global Value Chain Analysis: A primer*. Center on Globalization Governance and Competitiveness, May 31. Durham, N.C.: Duke University Press.

Gilley, B. (2012) 'Authoritarian environmentalism and China's response to climate change', *Environmental Politics*, 21(2), 287–307.

Gong, J. (2011) 'The crisis of cadmium rice', *Century Weekly* (in Chinese), February 14, 473. <http://magazine.caing.com/2011/cwcs437/> (accessed December 15, 2012).

Gou, Hongyang (2010) *The Low Carbon Plot: China's vital war with the US and Europe* (in Chinese). Taiyuan: Shanxi Economic Press.

Green Beagle (2011) 'Workshop held between environmental volunteers and CR Snow on Kekexili Protection', August 26. <http://news.lanbailan.com/html/2011/08/581314330689_1.shtml> (accessed December 15, 2012).

Green River (2012) 'The last moment of Durban', January 18. <www.greenriver.org/a/latest/2012/0118/303.html> (accessed December 15, 2012).

Gui, Y., Ma, W. and Muhlhahn, K. (2009) 'Grassroots transformation in contemporary China', *Journal of Contemporary Asia*, 39(3), 400–23.

Guo, L. (ed.) (2011) 'CR Snow's nationwide launch of "Brave to the World's End, Traversing beyond Kekexili" campaign', *People's Daily Online*, June 2. <http://shipin.people.com.cn/GB/14807930.html> (accessed December 15, 2012).

Hald, M. (2009) *Sustainable Urban Development and the Chinese Eco-City Concepts: Strategies, policies and assessments*. Lysaker, Norway: Fridtjof Nansen Institute.

Hall, Nina L. and Taplin, Ros (2007) 'Revolution or inch-by-inch? Campaign approaches on climate change by environmental groups', *Environmentalist*, 27, 95–107.

Hamlin, T. (2009) 'Resource exploitation in Southeast Asia: the unanticipated costs', in Richard Cronin and Amit Pandya (eds), *Exploiting National Resources: Growth, instability, and conflict in the Middle East and Asia*. Washington DC: Henry L. Stimson Centre.

Havel, V. (2007) 'Our moral footprint', *New York Times,* September 27. <www.nytimes.com/2007/09/27/opinion/27havel.html?_r=3&> (accessed December 15, 2012).

He, P. (2008) 'Mask wearing American athletes apologizes to the Chinese public', *Global Times* (in Chinese), August 6. <http://news.sina.com.cn/c/2008-08-06/204816073438.shtml> (accessed December 15, 2012).

Ho, Peter (2001) 'Greening without conflict? Environmentalism, NGOs and civil society in China', *Development and Change*, 32, 892–921.

Ho, Peter (2006) 'Trajectories for greening in China: theory and practice', *Development and Change*, 37(1), 3–28.

Ho, P. and Edmonds, R. L. (2008) *China's Embedded Activism: Opportunities and constraints of a social movement*. New York: Routledge.

Hong, D. Y. (2007) *The Growing Non-Governmental Forces for Environmental Protection in China* (in Chinese), Beijing: China Renmin University Press.

Hong Kong Trade Development Council (HKTDC) (2011) 'PDR economic profile', November 18. <http://china-trade-research.hktdc.com/business-news/article/Fast-Facts/PRD-Economic-Profile/ff/en/1/1X000000/1X06BW84.htm> (accessed December 15, 2012).

Hook, L. (2011) "China pollution "threat to growth"", *Financial Times*, February 28. <www.ft.com/cms/s/0/3671a476-4359-11e0-8f0d-00144feabdc0.html#axzz2H11Dxy00> (accessed December 15, 2012).

Hsu, Jennifer Y. J. and Hasmath, Reza (eds) (2012) *The Chinese Corporatist State: Adaption, survival and resistance*. London: Routledge.

Hu, A. G. (2002) *Strategy of China* (in Chinese), Hangzhou: Zhejiang People's Press.

Hu, A. G. and Liang, J. C. (2011) 'China's green era begins', pp. 17–21 in China Dialogue (eds), *China's Green Revolution: Energy, environment and the 12th Five-Year Plan*. Beijing: China Dialogue Report.

Hu, J. T. (2012) 'Hu Jintao's Report at the 18th Party Congress', *Xinhua Press*, November 17. <http://news.xinhuanet.com/english/special/18cpcnc/2012-11/17/c_131981259.htm> (accessed December 15, 2012).

Hu, Y. Q. (2010) 'Greenlaw and the first year of China's open environmental information regulations', pp. 211–15 in *China Environment Series 11*. Washington DC: Woodrow Wilson International Center for Scholars..

Huang, T. (2008) '"The true Hoh Xil", nation-wide photographic tour enters Yunan University', Education Channel of People, April 24. <http://edu.people.com.cn/GB/7161361.html> (accessed December 15, 2012).

International Energy Association (2012) *Oil and Gas Emergency Policy–China 2012 update*. <ww.iea.org/publications/freepublications/publication/name,28189,en.html> (accessed December 15, 2012).

Isaacson, Walter (2011) *Steve Jobs*, trans. Y. Q. Guan et al. Beijing: China Citic Press.

Isaacson, Walter (2012) *Steve Jobs*, trans. Y. J. Liao, X. Y. Jiang and K. D. Xie. Taipei: Commonwealth Publishing.

Jia, H. P. (2007) 'Global warming, science communication and public engagement—analysis of S&T Communication of climate change in China', *Science Popularization*, 3, 39–45.

Jiang, D. B. (2012) 'The public has a reason to thank American embassy monitoring PM2.5', *Netease News* opinion page, June 6. <http://news.163.com/special/reviews/airmonitor0606.html> (accessed December 15, 2012).

Jiang, G. M. (2006) 'Speak truth to power', in B. Y. Cao (ed.), *Journey of the Souls: Life of 36 Chinese contemporary scholars in their own words*. Beijing: Contemporary China Publishing House.

Jiang, G. M. (2007) 'Be aware of the green desert', *Environmental Economy* (in Chinese), 7, 38–41.

Jiang, X., Lv, Z., Shen, Q. and Yao, X. (2012) 'Front and back stage of the rainstorm warning', *Southern Weekly* (in Chinese), July 26. <www.infzm.com/content/78945> (accessed December 15, 2012).

Jin, Y. (2012a) 'More than 10 million texts sent in Beijing to warn of rainstorm', *Beijing News* (in Chinese), September 2. <http://news.sohu.com/20120902/n352125149.shtml> (accessed December 15, 2012).

Jin, Y. (2012b) 'PM2.5 monitor will be nationally employed by 2016', *Beijing News* (in Chinese), January 1. <http://news.sina.com.cn/c/2012-01-01/022723733101.shtml> (accessed December 15, 2012).

Jin, Y., Wen, X., Tang, Y., Liu, L., Guo, C. and Yao, P. (2012) 'Beijing Metrological Station claim one million text warnings sent', *Beijing News* (in Chinese), July 24. <http://news.sina.com.cn/c/2012-07-24/114724834273.shtml> (accessed December 15, 2012).

Jinghua Times (2012) 'Many well-known buildings flooded by rainstorm', *Jinghua Times* (in Chinese), August 6. <http://epaper.jinghua.cn/html/2012-08/06/content_893705.htm> (accessed December 15, 2012).

Johnson, H. and Noakes, J. A. (eds) (2005) *Frames of Protest: Social movements and the framing perspective*. Lanham, Md.: Rowman & Littlefield.

Johnson, Thomas (2010) 'Environmentalism and NIMBYism in China: promoting a rules-based approach to public participation', *Environmental Politics*, 19(3), 430–48.

Jones, D. (2009) 'China's Snow jumps Bud Light to be world no. 1', Reuters, March 31. <www.reuters.com/article/2009/03/31/beer-world-idUSLV64401920090331> (accessed December 15, 2012).

Kang, X. and Han, H. (2008) 'Graduated controls: the state-society relationship in contemporary China', *Modern China*, 34, 36–55.

Kay, T. (2011) 'Building solidarity with subjects and audience in sociology and documentary photography', *Sociological Forum*, 26, 424–30.

Knup, E. (1997) *Environmental NGOs in China: An overview*. Washington DC: Environmental Change and Security Program.

Lacey, S. (2011) 'How China dominates solar power', *Guardian* (UK), September 12. <www.guardian.co.uk/environment/2011/sep/12/how-china-dominates-solar-power> (accessed December 15, 2012).

Lampton, D. (1987) 'Chinese politics: the bargaining treadmill', *Issues and Studies*, 23, 13–20.

Landreth, J. (2011) 'Apple's China "suppliers" under fire for pollution', *AFP News*, September 1.

Lee, S. (2003) 'More players on the stage: new trends in Shanghai's water pollution control policies', pp. 110–15 in *China Environment Series 6*. Washington DC: Woodrow Wilson International Centre for Scholars.

Lei, S. and Qian, Y. (2004) 'Strategy and mechanism study for promotion of circular economy in China', *China Population Resources and Environment*, 2, 5–8.

Lema, A. (2007) 'Between fragmented authoritarianism and policy coordination: creating a Chinese market for wind energy', *Energy Policy*, 35(7), 3879–90.

Li, J. R. (2009) *Director of the Environment Bureau* (in Chinese). Beijing: People's Publishing House.

Li, K. Q. (2012) 'Develop a modern China with ecological progress', speech of vice premier of the State Council and chairman of CCICED Li Keqiang at the Opening Ceremony of CCICED 2012 Annual General Meeting, December 13. Beijing: CCICED. <http://cciced.net/encciced/event/AGM_1/2012agm/speeches2011/201212/t20121218_243944.html> (accessed December 15, 2012).

Li, R. R. (2013) 'Golf becomes a popular sport among Chinese kids, increases chance of entering American famous univeristies', *Xinmin Wanbao*, January 4. <http://sports.sohu.com/20130104/n362372969.shtml> (accessed December 15, 2012).

Li, X. M. (2010) 'US consumers demand a greener Apple for China', *Pacific Environment Blog*, July 19. <http://pacificenvironment.org/blog/2010/07/us-consumers-demand-a-greener-apple-for-china/> (accessed December 15, 2012).

Li, Y. (2010) 'High frequency of environmental pollution, who should the Chinese blame?' *China Business News* (in Chinese), August 3. <http://gongyi.163.com/10/0803/10/6D5GP0H100933KDH.html> (accessed December 15, 2012).

Li, Z. (2010) 'Silence from the responsible party of the Dalian pipe explosion, no words on compensation', *China News*, August 6. <http://news.sohu.com/20100806/n274021977.shtml> (accessed December 15, 2012).

Li, Z. M. (2011) 'Route may be off-limit, CR Snow "Courage Adventure" to Kekexili been questioned', *National Business Daily*, September 2. <http://old.nbd.com.cn/newshtml/20110902/2011090201385577.html> (accessed December 15, 2012).

Liao, X. Y. (2008) 'Review of the background of setting up the "Lehe Jiayuan" project', Lehe Jiayuan blogsite, October 2008. <http://blog.sina.com.cn/s/blog_6a1e72f20100l0my.html> (accessed December 15, 2012).

Lieberthal, K. (1992) 'The "fragmented authoritarianism" model and its limitations', pp. 1–30 in K. Lieberthal and D. Lampton (eds), *Bureaucracy, Politics, and Decision Making in Post-Mao China*. Berkeley, Calif.: University of California Press.

Lieberthal, K. G. and Lampton, D. M. (eds) (1992) *Bureaucracy, Politics, and Decision Making in Post-Mao China*. Berkeley, Calif.: University of California Press.

Lieberthal, K. and Oksenberg, M. (1988) *Policy Making in China: Leaders, structures, and processes*. Princeton, N.J.: Princeton University Press.

Liu, Fugang (2009) *Resource Utilization and Environmental Protection on Basis of Environmental Ethics* (in Chinese). Beijing: National Defense Industry Press.

Liu, J. (2012) '"Trash vegetable" attracts attention, experts claim southern soil facilitates plants' absorption of heavy metal', *Nanfang Daily*, December 26. <http://gd.people.com.cn/n/2012/1226/c123932-17920832.html> (accessed December 15, 2012).

Liu, L. G. (2011) 'Understanding China's climate change mitigation policy development: structures, processes and outcomes', FIU Electronic Theses and Dissertations, Paper 429.

Liu, Xuazaihui (2010) *In the Name of CO$_2$: Global rivalry behind the low carbon deceptions* (in Chinese). Beijing: China Development Press.

Liu, Y. (2012) 'iPhone 5 confronts labour shortage Henan massively subsides Foxconn', *China Business Journal*, September 22. <www.cb.com.cn/1634427/20120922/415028.html> (accessed December 15, 2012).

Lo, Alex Y. (2010) 'Active conflict or passive coherent? The political economy of climate change in China', *Environmental Politics*, 19(6), 1012–17.

Lo, C. W.-H., Fryxell, G. E. and Tang, S.-Y. (2010) 'Stakeholder pressures from perceived environmental impacts and the effect on corporate environmental management programmes in China', *Environmental Politics*,19(6), 888–909.

Lowe, T., Brown, K., Dessal, S., de Franca Doria, M., Haynes, K. and Vincent, K. (2006) 'Does tomorrow ever come? Disaster narrative and public perceptions of climate change', *Public Understanding of Science*, 15, 435–57.

Lu, Y.-Y. (2007) 'Environmental civil society and governance in China', *International Journal of Environmental Studies*, 64(1), 59–69.

Lv, J. B. and Zhang, Y. R. (2012) 'Private environment monitoring attracts passion, caution on interpreting data', *Xinmin News* (in Chinese), July 19. <http://xmwb.news365.com.cn/jd/201207/t20120719_540057.html> (accessed December 15, 2012).

Ma, Q. S. (2002) 'The governance of NGOs in China since 1978: how much autonomy?' *Nonprofit and Voluntary Sector Quarterly*, 31, 305–28.

Ma, Q. S. (2003) 'Nongovernmental and nonprofit organizations and the evolution of Chinese civil society', oral testimony at issue roundtable To Serve the People: NGOs and the Development of Civil Society in China. Congressional-Executive Commission on China.

Ma, Q. S. (2005) *Non-Governmental Organizations in Contemporary China: Paving the way to civil society?* London and New York: Routledge.

Ma, X. and Ortolano, L. (2000) *Environmental Regulation in China: Institutions, enforcement, and compliance.* Lanham, Md. and Oxford, England: Rowman & Littlefield.

Macur, J. (2008) 'U.S. cyclists are masked, and criticism is not', *New York Times*, August 6. <www.nytimes.com/2008/08/06/sports/olympics/06masks.html> (accessed December 15, 2012).

Madrigal, A. (2008) 'Why China's Olympian efforts to clean up Beijing's air won't work', *Wired*, July 15. <www.wired.com/wiredscience/2008/07/why-chinas-effo> (accessed December 15, 2012).

Marks, D. (2010) 'China's climate change policy process: improved but still weak and fragmented', *Journal of Contemporary China*, 19(67), 971–86.

Master, F (2010) 'Air pollution engulfs China's Shanghai after expo', Reuters, November 30. <www.reuters.com/article/2010/11/30/us-chian-pollution-idUSTRE6AT0W520101130> (accessed December 15, 2012).

Matus, K., Nam, K. M., Selir N. E., Lamsal, L. N., Reilly J. M. and Paltsev, S. (2012) 'Health damages from air pollution in China', *Global Environmental Change*, 22, 55–66.

McBeath, J. (2007) 'Discovering nature: globalization and environmental culture in China and Taiwan', *China Review International*, 14, 596–8.

Mertha, A. (2009) '"Fragmented authoritarianism 2.0": political pluralization in the Chinese policy process', *China Quarterly*, 200, 995–1012.

Mertha, A. (2010) 'Society in the state: China's nondemocratic political pluralisation', pp. 69–84 in P. Hays Gries and S. Rosen (eds), *Chinese Politics: State, society and the market*. London: Routledge.

Ministry of Environmental Protection (MEP) (2009) 'Communication on collecting suggestions on "Regulatory Rules on Environment Monitoring"', Communication no. 394. Beijing: MEP. <www.mep.gov.cn/info/bgw/bbgth/200905/t20090505_151174.htm> (accessed December 15, 2012).

MEP (2012) *Bulletin of China's Environmental Conditions*, June 6. Beijing: MEP.

Mol, P. J. and Carter, N. T. (2006) 'China's environmental governance in transition', *Environmental Politics*, 15(2), 149–70.

Moore, A. and Warren, A. (2006) 'Legal advocacy in environmental public participation in China: raising the stakes and strengthening stakeholders', pp. 2–23 in *China Environment Series*, Washington DC: Woodrow Wilson International Centre for Scholars.

Moore, M. (2009) 'China's "next leader" in hardline rant', *Telegraph*, February 16. <www.telegraph.co.uk/news/worldnews/asia/china/4637039/Chinas-next-leader-in-hardline-rant.html> (accessed December 15, 2012).

Nature University (2012) 'Open appeal to establishing Beidagang wetland national natural reserve with 10 suggestions', November 28. <www.nu.ngo.cn/plus/view.php?aid=464> (accessed December 15, 2012).

Ogden, S. (2004) 'From patronage to profits: the changing relationship of Chinese intellectuals with the party-state', in E. X. Gu and M. Goldman (eds), *Chinese Intellectuals Between State and Market*. London and New York: Routledge.

Olesen, A (2012) 'Tough questions after Beijing rain storm kills 37', Associated Press, July 23. <http://news.yahoo.com/tough-questions-beijing-rain-storm-kills-37-060950202.html> (accessed December 15, 2012).

Olivier, J. G. J., Janssens-Maenhout, G. and Peters, A. A. H. W. (2012) *Trend in Global CO$_2$ Emissions: 2012 report*. The Hague/Bilthoven, Netherlands: PBL Netherlands Environmental Assessment Agency.

Pan, X. T. (2012) 'Beijing is to publish new version of air quality control next year', *People's Daily* (overseas edition), September 12. <http://

nb.people.com.cn/n/2012/0912/c200879-17472068.html> (accessed December 15, 2012).

Papastergiadis, Nikos (2012) *Cosmopolitanism and Culture*. Cambridge: Polity Press.

Peking University Environment Science Centre (PUESC) (1999) *Overview of Air Pollution and Control Strategies in World's Ten Major Cities: No. 8, Qianxian* (in Chinese). <www.bjqx.org.cn/qxweb/n1766c192.aspx> (accessed December 15, 2012).

Peng, X. F. (2012) 'Chen Guangbiao launches canned fresh air', *Morning Post* (in Chinese), September 17 . <http://news.163. com/12/0917/02/8BIOBD1J00014AED.html> (accessed December 15, 2012).

Perry, E. J. and Selden M. (eds) (2000) *Chinese Society: Change, conflict, and resistance*, 2nd edn. New York: Routledge.

Pichler, F. (2012) 'Cosmopolitanism in a global perspective: an international comparison of open-minded orientations and identity in relation to globalization', *International Sociology*, 27(1), 21–50.

Preston, F. (2012) *A Global Redesign? Shaping the circular economy*. Briefing paper. London: Chatham House.

Qi, Y. (ed.) (2011) *Blue Book of Low-carbon Development: Annual review of low carbon development in China (2011–2012)*. Beijing: Social Science Academic Press.

Ramzy, A. (2012) 'Conflict in the air: US vows to keep reporting on pollution in China', *Time*, June 6. <http://world.time.com/2012/06/06/ conflict-in-the-air-u-s-will-keep-reporting-on-pollution-in-china/> (accessed December 15, 2012).

Rao, P. and Jin, Y. (2012) 'Beijing drainage met with skepticism again: five questions towards rain contingency', *Beijing News* (in Chinese), July 23. <http://hi.people.com.cn/n/2012/0723/c231187-17272227.html> (accessed December 15, 2012).

Rathzel, N. and Uzzell, D. (2009) 'Changing relations in global environmental change', *Global Environmental Change*, **19**, 326–35.

Ren, L. (2008) 'Report on qualitative research of Chinese scientific literacy survey by in-depth interview, 2007', *Science Popularization* (in Chinese), 3(6), 35-45.

Richards, J. P. and Heard, J. 2005 'European environmental NGOs: issues, resources and strategies in marine campaigns', *Environmental Politics*, **14**(1), 23–41.

Rong, F. (2010) 'Understandng developing country stances on post-2012 climate change negotiations: comparative analysis of Brazil, China, India, Mexico, and South Africa', *Energy Policy*, **38**, 4582–91.

Saich, T. (2010) *Governance and Politics of China*, 3rd edn. Basingstoke: Palgrave.

Sarre, P. and Jehlicka, P. (2007) 'Environmental movements in space-time: the Czech and Slovak republics from Stalinism to post-socialism', *Transactions of the Institute of British Geographers*, **32**(3), 346–62.

Savitz, E. (2012) 'China's mobile market tops 1 billion subs; bullish for Apple', *Forbes Online*. <www.forbes.com/sites/ericsavitz/2012/04/27/chinas-mobile-market-tops-1-billion-subs-bullish-for-apple/> (accessed December 15, 2012).

Schroeder, M. (2008) 'The construction of China's climate politics: transnational NGOs and the spiral model of international relations', *Cambridge Review of International Affairs*, 21(4), 505–25.

Schroeder, M. (2009) 'Varieties of Carbon Governance: Utilizing the Clean Development Mechanism for Chinese Priorities', *Journal of Environment Development*, 18(4), 371-394

Schwartz, J. (2004) 'Environmental NGOs in China', *Pacific Affairs*, 77(1), 28–49.

Shan, J. and Wang, Q. (2011) 'Exposure to smog is severe hazard', *China Daily*, December 6. <www.chinadaily.com.cn/usa/china/2011-12/06/content_14216543.htm (accessed February 14, 2013).

Shapiro, J. (2001) *Mao's War Against Nature: Politics and the environment in revolutionary China*. Cambridge: Cambridge University Press.

Shapiro, J. (2012) *China's Environmental Challenges*. Cambridge: Polity.

Shearman, D. and Smith, J. W. (2007) *The Climate Change Challenge and the Failure of Democracy.* Westport, Conn.: Praeger.

Shen, W. (2011) 'Understanding the dominance of unilateral CDM projects in China: origins and implications for governing carbon market', Governance of Clean DevelopmentWorking Paper 016, July. Norwich: University of East Anglia. <www.tyndall.ac.uk/sites/default/files/gcd_workingpaper016.pdf > (accessed December 15, 2012).

Shin, S. (2010) 'The domestic side of the clean development mechanism: the case of China', *Environmental Politics*, 19(2), 237–54.

Smith, N. W. and Joffe, H. (2009) 'Climate chance in the British press: the role of the visual', *Journal of Risk Research*, 12(5), 647–63.

Song, Q., Huang, J-S., Song, X-J., Wang, X.-D. and Liu, Y. (2009) *Unhappy China: The great time, grand vision and our challenges* (in Chinese). Nanjing: Jiangsu People's Press.

Sontag, S. (1977) *On Photography*. London: Penguin.

Spencer, R. (2008) 'Beijing smog returns after Olympics,' *Telegraph* (UK), September 21. <www.telegraph.co.uk/news/worldnews/asia/china/3043321/Beijing-smog-returns-after-Olympics.html> (accessed December 15, 2012).

Sprinz, D. and Vaahtorant, T. (1994) 'The interest-based explanation of international environmental policy'. *International Organization*, 148(11), 77–105.

Stanway, D. (2010) 'China oil spill could be 60,000 metric tons: Greenpeace', Reuters, July 30. <www.reuters.com/article/2010/07/30/us-china-dalian-oil-idUSTRE66T2LQ20100730> (accessed December 15, 2012).

State Forestry Administration of China (SFA) (2011) *Bird-Watching in Mainland China* (in Chinese), April 7. Beijing: SFA Information Office.

Swartz, S. and Oster, S. (2010) 'China tops U.S. in energy use', *Wall Street*

Journal, July 18. <http://online.wsj.com/article/SB1000142405274870 372050457537671235315310.html> (accessed December 15, 2012).

Szymanski, T. (2006) 'China's take on climate change, sustainable development', *Ecosystems and Climate Change Committee Newsletter*, 9(1), 2–8.

Tan, Y.-F. and Zhou, F. (2005) 'The message behind oil shortage: building a energy-saving society is a must', *Nanfang Daily*, September 21. <www.southcn.com/news/gdnews/zhzt/youhuang/pinglun/200509210330.htm> (accessed December 15, 2012).

Tang, Shuiyan and Zhan, Xueyong (2008) 'Civic environmental NGOs, civil society and democratization in China', *Journal of Development Studies*, 44(3), 425–48.

Toner, M. (2012) US Department of State daily press briefing. June 6. Washington, DC: US Department of State.

Tong, J. (2012) 'Air quality cannot solely rely on official monitoring,' *Netease News*, June 6. <http://news.163.com/12/0606/18/83B90FQ S00012Q9L.html> (accessed December 15, 2012).

Tong, Y. Q. (2007) 'Bureaucracy meets the environment: elite perceptions in six cities', *China Quarterly*, 189, 112–16.

Touraine, Alain (1988) *Return of the Actor: Social theory in postindustrial society*. Minneapolis, Minn.: University of Minnesota Press.

Tsang, S. and Kolk, A. (2010) 'The evolution of Chinese policies and governance structures on environment, energy and climate', *Environmental Policy and Governance*, 20, 180–96.

Tschang, C.-C. (2007) 'China aims to clean up in solar power', *Bloomberg Businessweek*, April 11. <www.businessweek.com/stories/2007-04-11/ china-aims-to-clean-up-in-solar-powerbusinessweek-business-news-stock-market-and-financial-advice> (accessed December 15, 2012).

United Nations (2012) *World Urbanization Prospects*. New York: United Nations.

United Nations Environment Programme (UNEP) (2009) *UNEP Report Spotlights Achievements and Highlights Some Shortcomings of 2008 Games*. 25th Session of UNEP's Governing Council/Global Ministerial Environment Forum, February16–20. Nairobi: UNEP.

Van der Heijden, H. (1999) 'Environmental movements, ecological modernisation and political opportunity structures', *Environmental Politics*, 8(1), 199–221.

Van der Slot, A. and van den Berg, W. (2012) *Clean Energy, Living Planet:The race to the top of global clean energy technology manufacturing* (report commisioned by WWF-Netherlands). Amesterdam: Roland Berger Strategy Consultants.

Waddock, S. (2011) 'We are all stakeholders of Gaia: a normative perspective on stakeholder thinking', *Organization Environment*, 24, 192–212.

Waldmeir, P., Hook, L. and Anderlini, J. (2012) 'Ningbo protest, response both typical of China's environmental debate', *Washington Post*, October 29. <http://articles.washingtonpost.com/2012-10-29/

world/35499496_1_ningbo-environmental-protesters-toxic-chemical-spill> (accessed February 21, 2013).

Wang, D.-M. (2002) 'Seize the opportunity, face the challenge, coordinate development and achieve "human–nature unity"', *Resources and Environment in the Yangtze Basin* (in Chinese), **11**(4), 327–31.

Wang, Feng (2008) *Research on Action Mechanism in Public Participation in Environmental Protection* (*Gongzhong canyu huanbao xingwei jili yanjiu*). Beijing: China Environmental Science Press.

Wang, G. M. and Luo, H. X. (2011) 'New perspective on agricultural labour force research: the theory and empirical analysis of "kongxinhua"', *Rural Economy* (in Chinese), **12**, 108–11.

Wang, H. (2010) 'Documentary on Dalian crude oil spill', *CBN Weekly* (in Chinese), August 5. <http://news.ifeng.com/mainland/special/dalianyouguanbaozha/content-2/detail_2010_08/05/1894144_0.shtml> (accessed December 15, 2012).

Wang, H. and Chen, M. L. (2006) 'China civil environment movement: the third force is struggling forward', *Xinhua News*, October 20. <http://news.xinhuanet.com/environment/2006-10/20/content_5226743.htm> (accessed December 15, 2012).

Wang, J. (2012) 'Listen to Zhong Nanshan speaking the truth', *Beijing Youth Weekly Times*, 858, 12–15.

Wang, K. and Luo, X. (2012) 'Parts of Baiyangdian suffer loss from fish death,' *Xinhua News*, August 16. <http://news.xinhuanet.com/tech/2012-08/16/c_123587831.htm> (accessed December 15, 2012).

Wang, L. P. (2007) 'China's half century detour of afforestation' (in Chinese), *Scientific Times*, August 21. <http://news.sciencenet.cn/sbhtmlnews/20078220322750187506.html?id=18750> (accessed December 15, 2012).

Wang, S. S. (ed.) (2012) 'Ministry of Environment Protection: hope certain consulate in China stop publishing air quality information,' *China News*, June 5. <http://finance.chinanews.com/ny/2012/06-05/3939606.shtml> (accessed December 15, 2012).

Wang, Shu (2012) '29% of annual increase of environmental public event, less than 1% of legal intervention', *Beijing News* (in Chinese), October 27. <http://news.qq.com/a/20121027/000067.htm> (accessed December 15, 2012).

Wang, Shuo (2012) 'MEP: civil environment monitor not been restricted'. *Beijing Times*, July 17. <http://news.xinhuanet.com/local/2012-07/17/c_123420987.htm> (accessed December 15, 2012).

Wang, X. (2011) 'Beijing Apple store conflict attracts foreign media attention, claiming Chinese going mad for the products', *Global Times* (in Chinese), May 9. <http://world.huanqiu.com/roll/2011-05/1679661.html> (accessed December 15, 2012).

Wang, X. Y. (2005) 'The grand energy issue, irrelevant to you and me?' *Nanfang Daily*, September 21. <www.southcn.com/news/gdnews/zhzt/youhuang/pinglun/200509210246.htm> (accessed December 15, 2012).

Wang, Y. (2006) 'Investigation on Baiyangdian's fish death: Industrial waste water held accountable', China Central Television *Oriental Times*, April 10. <http://news.eastday.com/eastday/node81741/node81762/node128811/userobject1ai1971749.html> (accessed December 15, 2012).

Watts, J. (2009) 'China puts its faith in solar power with huge renewable energy investment', *Guardian* (UK), May 26. <www.guardian.co.uk/world/2009/may/26/china-invests-solar-power-renewable-energy-environment> (accessed December 15, 2012).

Watts, J. (2010) *When a Billion Chinese Jump: How China will save mankind – or destroy it.* New York: Scribner.

Watts, J. (2012) 'China resorts to blackouts in pursuit of energy efficiency', *Guardian* (UK), September 19. <www.guardian.co.uk/world/2010/sep/19/china-blackouts-energy-efficiency> (accessed December 15, 2012).

Watts, J., Carrington, D. and Goldenberg, S. (2010) 'China's fears of rich nation "climate conspiracy" at Copenhagen revealed', *Guardian* (UK), February 11. <www.guardian.co.uk/environment/2010/feb/11/chinese-thinktank-copenhagen-document> (accessed December 15, 2012).

Wei, D. S. (2010) 'Chen Guangbiao: aimed to be China's leading rich and philanthropist', *Zijing News*, October 11. <www.zijing.org/gongyi/html/?70578.html> (accessed December 15, 2012).

Wei, L. M. (2007) 'Guangdong: oil shortage or oil panicking?' *Economic Observer* (in Chinese), November 3. <http://finance.sina.com.cn/g/20071103/00204134198.shtml> (accessed December 15, 2012).

Wheeler, K. and Nauright, J. (2006) 'A global perspective on the environmental impact of golf', *Sport in Society*, 9(3), 427–43.

Whiting, S. H. (1991) 'The politics of NGO development in China', *Voluntas*, 2(2), 16–48.

Whittington, J. (2004) 'China facing environment "crisis"', *BBC News Online*, September 23. <http://news.bbc.co.uk/1/hi/world/asia-pacific/3683574.stm> (accessed December 15, 2012).

World Bank (2009a) *World Development Report 2010: Development and climate change*, November 6. Washington DC: World Bank.

World Bank (2009b) *Sino-Singapore Tianjin Eco-City: A case study of an emerging eco-city in China.* Technical Assistance Report, November. Washington DC: World Bank.

World Bank and State Environmental Protection Administration, P. R. China (2007) *Cost of Pollution in China: Economic estimates of physical damages*, February. Washington DC: World Bank.

World Commission on Environment and Development (1987) *Our Common Future.* Oxford: Oxford University Press.

World Resource Institute (1999) *China's Health and Environment: Air pollution and health effects.* Washington DC: World Resource Institute.

Wu, D. (2012) 'Suanlitun Apple store cancels iphone 4s sale due to chaos', *Sina Tech*, January 13. <http://tech.sina.com.cn/t/2012-01-13/08136635347.shtml> (accessed December 15, 2012).

Wu, J. (2009) 'Unhappy China venders ill nationalism', *China Youth*

Daily, April 8. <http://news.xinhuanet.com/book/2009-04/08/content_11149190_2.htm> (accessed December 15, 2012).

Wu, J. (2012) 'Metrology Station: warning texts will not charge', *Southern Weekly* (in Chinese), August 1. <www.infzm.com/content/79142> (accessed December 15, 2012).

Wu, T. (2011) 'Our air quality cannot be perceived through American embassy's monitor', *Morning Post* (in Chinese), November 1. <www.chinanews.com/gn/2011/11-01/3427307.shtml> (accessed December 15, 2012).

Wu, Z. Y. (ed.) (2012) '*A Bit of China* stirred up homesickness among overseas Chinese', *China Youth International*, May 25. <http://news.youth.cn/wzpd/201205/t20120525_2195725.htm> (accessed December 15, 2012).

Xiao, C. F. and Xu, Y. J. (2008) 'Du Shaozhong: China can guaranttee good air quality during the Olympics', *Xinhua News Press*. <www.gov.cn/jrzg/2008-07/26/content_1056511.htm> (accessed December 15, 2012).

Xie, Xiaoping (2011) 'Apple wakes up to Chinese pollution concerns', *Guardian* (UK), October 4. <www.guardian.co.uk/environment/2011/oct/04/apple-chinese-pollution-concerns> (accessed December 15, 2012).

Xinhua (2009) 'China to further develop solar energy', *China Daily*, January 26. <www.chinadaily.com.cn/china/2009-01/26/content_7429080.htm> (accessed December 15, 2012).

Xinhua (2012a) 'China's mobile phone users hit 1.1 bln', *Xinhua News*, November 29. <http://news.xinhuanet.com/english/china/2012-11/29/c_132008002.htm [Accessed 15 December 2012].

Xinhua (2012b) 'China's imported oil dependence continues rise', Xinhua News, May 10. <http://news.xinhuanet.com/english/china/2012-05/10/c_131580559.htm> (accessed December 15, 2012).

Xu, J. and Wan, F. (2008) 'An analysis of the evolution stages of the grassroots environmental NGOs in China', *Comparative Economic and Social System* (in Chinese), **136**, 164–9.

Xun, D. (ed.) (2011) 'Experts state PM2.5 incompatible with Chinese economic and environment and lacks international standards,' *Morning Post* (in Chinese), November 12. <www.china.com.cn/news/txt/2011-11/12/content_23892612.htm> (accessed December 15, 2012).

Yan, M. and Lin, P. (2011) 'Xie Zhenhua's rage over Western countries: What entitles you to lecture us here?' Phoenix Satellite Television, December 11. <http://news.ifeng.com/world/special/deban/content-3/detail_2011_12/11/11246538_0.shtml> (accessed December 15, 2012).

Yan, Y. L. (2012) 'Heavy metal pollution sporadic in north dense in south, MEP planning for 30 billion soil repair', *People's Daily Online*, June 28. <http://env.people.com.cn/n/2012/0628/c1010-18403483.html> (accessed December 15, 2012).

Yang, G. B. (2005) 'Environmental NGOs and institutional dynamics in China', *China Quarterly*, **181**, 46–66.

Yang, G. B. (2009) 'Civic environmentalism', in Hsing Youtien and Ching

Kwan Lee (eds), *Reclaiming Chinese Society: The new social activism*. London: Routledge.

Yang, J. P. (2011) 'Afforestation, greening the motherland: a study of Mao Zedong's thoughts on forestry', *China Forestry* (in Chinese), January 18. <www.greentimes.com/green/news/cxlh/lhby/content/2011-01/18/content_115921.htm> (accessed December 15, 2012).

Yang, X. M. (2011) 'Over half Chinese living in urban areas', *People's Daily*, December 20. <http://english.people.com.cn/90882/7682623.html> (accessed December 15, 2012).

Yi, F., He, G. and Liu, X. (2012) 'Volunteers call for upgraded protection in "Beidagang"', *Beijing News* (in Chinese), November 29. <www.bjnews.com.cn/news/2012/11/29/236380.html> (accessed December 15, 2012).

Yi, F. and Liu, X. (2012) 'Experts advise Beidagang to be upgraded to national natural reserve', *Beijing News* (in Chinese), November 26. <www.bjnews.com.cn/news/2012/11/26/235766.html> (accessed December 15, 2012).

Yi, Y. (2011) 'CR Snow traversing Kekexili, environmental volunteer to stop onsite', China Internet Information Center. <http://news.china.com.cn/txt/2011-10/18/content_23653365.htm> (accessed December 15, 2012).

Yuan, Z., Bi, J. and Moriguichi, Y. (2006) 'The circular economy: a new development strategy in China', *Journal of Industrial Ecology*, 10, 4–8.

Zbicz, D. C. (2009) *Asia's Future: Critical thinking for a changing environment*, September. Washington DC: Woodrow Wilson International Center for Scholars.

Zhang, F. Y. (2012) 'Chen Guangbiao selling air is not just performing art', *Guangzhou Daily*, August 13. <http://news.xinhuanet.com/comments/2012-08/13/c_112705267.htm> (accessed December 15, 2012).

Zhang, H. (2012) 'MEP denies ban on civil monitor of PM2.5 claiming regulation revision still in process', *Beijing Evening News*, July 18. <http://gongyi.people.com.cn/n/2012/0718/c151650-18542025.html> (accessed December 15, 2012).

Zhang, J., Mauserall, D., Zhu, T., Liang, S., Essati, M. and Remais, J. V. (2010) 'Environmental health in China: Progress towards clean air and safe water', *Lancet*, 375, 1110–19.

Zhang, J. and Meng, F. (2012) 'Baiyangdian 2000 acres water clear of fish in three days', *Jinghua Times*, August 27. <http://politics.people.com.cn/n/2012/0827/c70731-18836287.html> (accessed December 15, 2012).

Zhang, J. Y. (2011) 'Scientific institutions and effective governance: a case study of Chinese stem cell research', *New Genetics and Society*, 30(2), 193–207.

Zhang, J. Y. (2012) *The Cosmopolitanization of Science: Stem cell governance in China*. Basingstoke: Palgrave Macmillan.

Zhang, L. (2011) 'Jobs: from beginning to the end', *Lens* (in Chinese), 10, 26–48.

Zhang, L. (2012) 'Hometown on the tongue, in the periodic table or under the bulldozer,' *Beijing Evening News*, May 25. <http://opinion.people.com.cn/GB/17986288.html> (accessed December 15, 2012).

Zhang, L.-H. (2011) 'New China's early explorations of environmental protection: Chinese government's environmental efforts before the first national environment protection conference', *Contemporary China History Studies* (in Chinese), 4, 40–7.

Zhang, X. C. (2009) 'First week battle at Copenhagen: China is not happy', *China Times*, December 11. <http://finance.sina.com.cn/roll/20091211/21277093241.shtml> (accessed December 15, 2012).

Zhang, Z., Zhang, X., Song, Q., Tang, Z., Qiao, B. and Gu, Q. (1996) *China Can Say No: Political and emotional choices in the post cold-war era*. Beijing: China Industry & Commerce Associated Press

Zhao, Q. M. (2009) 'American embassy keeps close watch on Beijing air. Foreign media focus on Beijing air pollution again,' *World News Journal* (in Chinese), July 1. <http://gb.cri.cn/27824/2009/07/01/3245s2551082.htm> (accessed December 15, 2012).

Zhao, W. and Wan, Y. (2012) 'Who will protect Beijing's dissapearing swallow?', *Xinhua News Press,* November. <http://roll.sohu.com/20121102/n356553406.shtml> (accessed December 15, 2012).

Zhao, X. (2012) 'Forthcoming lecture, 17 October 2012', *BirdWatch China*, October 13. <www.cbw.org.cn/forums//viewthread.php?tid=165155&sid=17GfZr> (accessed December 15, 2012).

Zheng, Y. N. and Sow, K. T. (2007*) Harmonious Society and Harmonious World: China's policy discourse under Hu Jintao,* Brief Paper 26. Nottingham: China Policy Institute.

Zhong, S. (2012) 'Green development testifies China's capacity of taking actions', *People's Daily*, July 23. <http://opinion.people.com.cn/n/2012/0723/c1003-18572731.html> (accessed December 15, 2012).

Zhuang, G.(2006) 'Role of China in global carbon market', *China and World Economy*, **14**(5), 93–108.

Legislation

Ministry of Land and Resources, People's Republic of China (1999) Marine Environment Protection Law of the People's Republic of China. Promulgated by Order No.26 of the President of the People's Republic of China on December 25, 1999.

State Council, People's Republic of China (1994) Regulation of the People's Republic of China on Nature Reserves. Promulgated by Order No. 167 of the State Council of People's Republic of China on 9 October 1994.

State Council, People's Republic of China (2007) Regulation of the People's Republic of China on the Disclosure of Government Information. Promulgated by Order No. 482 of the State Council of People's Republic of China on 5 April 2007.

State Environmental Protection Administration (2007) Measures for the Disclosure of Environmental Information (for Trial Implementation).

Promulgated by Order No. 35 of the State Environmental Protection
Administration on 21 April 2007.

Websites

2005 Pearl River Delta oil shortage: <www.southcn.com/news/gdnews/zhzt/youhuang/>

2007 Pearl River Delta oil shortage: <http://gd.xinhuanet.com/ztbd/youqi/>

7-21 Beijing Rain Storm page: <http://english.people.com.cn/102775/205678/index.html>

A Bite of China:

Bird Watch China: <www.cbw.org.cn/main.php>

Collective Lens: <www.collectivelens.com>

Chen Faqing (environmental activist):<www.nmcfq.com/about.asp>

China Bird Watching Network: <www.chinabirdnet.org>

Crowd-funding websites: Dianming Shijian: <http://demohour.com> and Youfu: <http://yoopay.cn>

Dalian 2010 oil spill: <http://news.sohu.com/s2010/youguanbaozha/ also see: http://news.163.com/photoview/3R710001/10169.html#p=6CKGAF023R710001>

Green Choice Alliance (China): <www.ipe.org.cn/alliance/ngo.aspx>

Green River: <www.green-river.org>

Green Long March Progamme: <www.future.org/international-operations/china/green-long-march> (in English) and <http://china.future.org/zh-hans/> (in Chinese)

History of Climate Negotiations in 83 seconds: <www.youtube.com/watch?v=B11kASPfYxY>

Low Carbon Conspiracy translation: <http://ourmaninsichuan.wordpress.com/2010/11/15/low-carbon-plot-or-why-cancun-has-already-failed/>

Netease News on air monitoring: <http://news.163.com/special/reviews/airmonitor0606.html>

Ma Jun's page, the Goldman Environmental Prize: <www.goldmanprize.org/recipient/ma-jun>

Pacific Environment: <www.pacificenvironment.org>

Snow Beer brand campaign: <http://yongchuang.snowbeer.com.cn/>

US Embassy Beijing Air Quality Monitor Site: <http://beijing.usembassy-china.org.cn/070109air.html>

Xie Zhenhua rage at Durban: <http://news.ifeng.com/world/special/deban/content-3/detail_2011_12/11/11246538_0.shtml>

INDEX